WHAT PEOPLE ARE SAYING ABOUT

AWARENESS IS ᴛ

Dr Itai Ivtzan elucidates not only ⟨...⟩ ⟨...⟩ᴄᴛ
psychology and spirituality but th ⟨...⟩ ᴀᴜᴅ power of the
two. Allow this accomplished scholar and meditator to offer you
this clear road-map as you take this journey to your indwelling.
This important book, peppered with research studies, validated
psychological tests, and practical exercises, offers clear and
insightful methods for you to re-discover your mindfulness and
hence...your freedom.

Dr Ryan M. Niemiec, author of *Mindfulness and Character
Strengths: A Practical Guide to Flourishing*, and education director
of the VIA Institute on Character

Dr Ivtzan has done a great service to humanity with this
beautiful book. Here we have two of our most precious currents
of thought, psychology and spirituality, each of which has transformed people's lives for the better, but which until now have
remained wary of each other. However, with great skill and
artistry, Dr. Ivtzan has brought these together in a 'marriage,' a
union which serves to greatly enrich both partners. Moreover, Dr
Ivtzan is just the kind of wise and compassionate pastor that we
need to skillfully conduct such a union, with his great depths of
insight and beauty of expression. However, the most important
beneficiary of this 'marriage' is the reader, who is invited to
embark upon their own personal journal of transformation.
Through a series of 'lessons,' including structured reflections
and exercises, the fortunate reader is led gently down a path of
mystery, towards realms of the self and of the universe that they
may not have suspected existed. Truly, this book has the power

to change your life.
Dr Tim Lomas, author of *Masculinity, Meditation and Mental Health*

Awareness Is Freedom provides a clear and practical course in spiritual training. It's an ideal introduction that quickly takes the reader from the shallows to the depths. Save yourself the trouble of learning Sanskrit, Pali or Tibetan in order to read the ancient sutras. Instead, I would advise you start your journey with this illuminating and accessible book. I wish I had had the opportunity to read it years ago before I wandered off to the East.
Tim Ward, author of *What the Buddha Never Taught: A 'Behind the Robes' Account of life in a Thai Forest Monastery*

Dr Itai Ivtzan draws on his vast amount of personal and professional knowledge to give readers insight into a very powerful topic area in an incredibly approachable way. Ivtzan is indeed a pioneer and leader in the field and his humour, wisdom and creativity will challenge readers, in so many ways. The book is engaging, stimulating and thought provoking as Ivtzan passionately melds theory with personal exercises and reflection sections.
Dr Kata Hefferon, author of *Positive Psychology and the Body: The somatopsychic side to flourishing*

Awareness
Is Freedom

The Adventure of Psychology and Spirituality

Awareness
Is Freedom

The Adventure of Psychology and Spirituality

Dr Itai Ivtzan

**CHANGE
MAKERS
BOOKS**

Winchester, UK
Washington, USA

First published by Changemakers Books, 2015
Changemakers Books is an imprint of John Hunt Publishing Ltd., Laurel House, Station Approach,
Alresford, Hants, SO24 9JH, UK
office1@jhpbooks.net
www.johnhuntpublishing.com
www.changemakers-books.com

For distributor details and how to order please visit the 'Ordering' section on our website.

Text copyright: Itai Ivtzan 2014

ISBN: 978 1 78279 851 4

A CIP catalogue record for this book is available from the British Library.

Design: Stuart Davies

Printed and bound by CPI Group (UK) Ltd, Croydon, CR0 4YY, UK

We operate a distinctive and ethical publishing philosophy in all
areas of our business, from our global network of authors to
production and worldwide distribution.

CONTENTS

Gratitude

Everything that I am, including this book, is so much more beautiful thanks to those who are part of my journey.

To Roy, Alon, Ori, and Yair; this book began with you guys.

To Aria; you nourished us with endless wisdom and love.

To my students; learning from you is truly a gift.

To Kate Hefferon and Tim Lomas; it is a privilege to share what others call "work" and we call "play".

To Tova Shany; your editing work and brilliant mind transformed this book. Without your work, this book would have been but a shadow of what it is.

To my mother Ilana and brother Ohad; I am grateful for the roots, support, and caring. Our love is precious.

To Netta and Aria; you are my family, and I love you with all my heart.

To life; thank you for inviting me. It is a great joy to participate in your game.

To the reader

Our story begins with my search for answers, before I realised that no one was able to provide me with the answers I was looking for, and the best they could do was help me refine my questions. I was driven to better understand two issues that seemed very important: "who am I?" and "why am I here?" People might regard these questions as impractical in nature and irrelevant to life, but I am convinced they are deeply meaningful and have an enormous influence on our lives. In my opinion, these two simple questions promise to generate tools to deal with life in a way that would prove profoundly right.

The next stage involved searching for paradigms to support me in my journey down the rabbit hole. I have spent long years studying, travelling the world, listening to lectures conceived in the most fascinating minds, and conferring with great teachers in monasteries. These experiences revealed to me the power of psychology and spirituality. I discovered the amazing knowledge and depth they both offered, and the wonderful way in which they support our growth process. But it also became obvious that the two were irreconcilable; it was almost as if they were perceived as rivals, as contrasting ways to understand life that could never converge. In the academic milieu, where I have been teaching and conducting research, spirituality was frequently frowned upon, perceived as esoteric and metaphysical, a sphere that could not be part of the scientific realm. At the same time, whenever I associated with spiritual groups, participated in *satsang*s (talks conducted by spiritual teachers with their disciples), and spent time in spiritual retreats, science and psychology seemed out of place. In these encounters, the mind and its processes were frequently regarded as symbolic enemies, and psychology, which represented them, was not welcome.

I was torn; whatever group I was part of lacked certain aspects that were available in the other group. The feeling that something was missing spurred me to start my own work, my own personal journey, and merge the teachings of both the psychological and spiritual worlds. The results were amazing: With time, I felt increasingly liberated. I became better acquainted with my authentic self and began to understand my role in the play called life.

This understanding has been woven since into different spheres of my work. A growing number of university classes I have been giving include spiritual topics. I have seen students who had been disappointed with their psychology studies come alive, a sparkle lighting their eyes when they found out that the psychology curriculum included spiritual topics. Spiritual issues were also integrated into my academic research. Several studies I have been conducting explore questions concerning wellbeing, psychology, and spirituality. The meditation retreats I run incorporate psychological theories and practices that enrich the experience. This winning combination is also applied to my therapeutic work; I have designed a therapeutic experience called AMT (Awareness Meaning Therapy), based upon a psychological process in which the clients explore in depth the meaning of their own lives, in a way that is strongly associated with the spiritual experience.

Over the years, I have frequently heard the words "this class/course/session/retreat has changed my life". This convinced me that my approach was highly effective, and was truly capable of changing one's life.

I am well aware that every aspect of my professional and personal life reflects the marriage between psychology and spirituality. In this book I wish to share this marriage with you. In spite of the challenges and difficulties of this experience, it is likely to transform your life if you approach it with dedication and love. The transformation may be different from what you expect and predict, and yet it will always be precisely what you need. I hope the information and exercises in this book invite you to grow, recognize your true self, and experience the depth of authentic joy and freedom.

Itai Ivtzan

Introduction

In this book, theoretical knowledge and practical exercises are combined in a way that inspires self-growth, and enhances awareness. As your awareness expands, you will develop the ability, and find the inner-space and the time to stop automatic conditioned reactions. Once you engage in this process and devote yourself to it, you will discover that your life has completely changed, and you have become more alert, sensitive, caring, alive, and connected to your own self and to others. The teachings put forward in this book are pyramid shaped, to assist you in achieving this deep transformation. The first couple of lessons lay the foundations for the journey to come. With each additional lesson we move closer to the pinnacle of this spiritual journey: freedom. The book is structured as a coherent journey that begins with *recognising* the illusion and the shackles that hold you down. It then guides you gradually and teaches you how to *let go*, abandon the illusion and release the shackles. It is recommended that you read the lessons by their order of appearance, as each lesson introduces ideas that fundamentally enhance the understanding of the following ones.

Lesson 1 introduces and explains the meeting point between psychology and spirituality, and the important role they both play in our journey towards freedom. It also discusses the ego and its influence. The exercises you will be asked to perform will show you how to recognise the concepts instilled in your ego, and the way these concepts interfere with your everyday life.

Lesson 2 introduces the practical skill that leads to liberation: meditation. We discuss the meaning of meditation, its effects, and its relevance for the spiritual journey. The practical exercises will assist you in exploring the mind's tendency to fluctuate, and will teach you an important meditation technique.

Lesson 3 focuses on your thinking experience. We discuss the difficulty arising from obsessive thinking, the difference between aware and unaware thinking, and ways to nurture one's aware thinking. In this lesson we also begin to understand the meaning of non-reactive attention and its power to break existing patterns. The practical exercises encourage you to develop new relations with your thinking process, and foster awareness so as to detach yourself from your thoughts.

Lesson 4 discusses the idea of *Ego Formed Self* and the way you adhere to it. It explains why it is an illusion, and how it creates a gap between your awareness and your life. Focus is placed on an alternative experience, that of an Authentic Self, and the issue of enlightenment is explored. The practical exercises proposed in this lesson aim to develop your awareness, deepen your practice of meditation, and reveal unknown depths of your reality.

Lesson 5 describes the neutral aspect of life, and shows that every moment is an open space distorted by personal perceptions that are injected into it. In this lesson, the practical exercises invite you to recognise situations where your mind distorts neutral moments, and acknowledge the resulting emotional effect.

Lesson 6 deals with the spiritual concept of *presence* and discusses a variety of meditation techniques that invite presence. By getting acquainted with different meditation techniques, you will be able to determine which of them is best suited to you. The practical exercises introduce you to eight meditation techniques; you will be asked to choose one of them and practice it over the week.

In lesson 7, the issue of *impermanence* is introduced. Understanding impermanence is essential as it helps you realise how futile attachment is. This lesson also explains the difference between dependent and independent emotions, and the effect each type has on your personal journey. The practical exercises will uncover your outlook on change, to allow for a more accepting attitude towards the inevitable changes in your life.

Lesson 8 explains the connection between your thoughts and emotions, and the way they revitalise each other. A link is then shown to exist between emotions and bodily sensations. This understanding extends the ability to attain meditative awareness, and provides an important tool for growth. The practical exercises bring these concepts together by means of a new meditation technique. They create an experiential link between the events in your life and the thoughts, emotions, and bodily sensations that accompany them.

As already mentioned, in each lesson you will be asked to perform exercises that are connected with the discussed topic. These exercises are tremendously important; students who have practiced them affirmed that they had a powerful impact on their spiritual journey and their life. We have to bear in mind that this journey for change and awareness requires much attention and dedication, and should combine equal shares of theory and practice. Practice must be based on knowledge. If the background, purpose, and value of an exercise are not clear, the exercise would be hard to perform with dedication. On the other hand, acquiring theoretical knowledge without applying it in practice would not bring about the desired transformation. Discussing a subject is an important starting point but it would come to nothing if it is not experienced in practice. Transformation will not occur by talking about change, but by actually making a change. The exercises are designed to create a personal experience that will sharpen your awareness and further your acknowledgment of your authentic self. You may read about the most profound theories and ideas, but they remain foreign and do not belong to you until you have actually applied them in your own life. Practice paves the way for you to own the ideas described in this book. It connects you to your ego concepts, improves your meditation technique, and develops your awareness and self-growth, to generate change. Read the ideas, contemplate their meaning, and experience the exercises –

this is the triangle offered in this book to achieve the desired transformation.

The exercises are divided into "Here and now" exercises and weekly exercises. The first are on-the-spot experiments you can try while you are reading. They are intended to instantly illustrate the idea being discussed. Weekly exercises are assignments derived from the topic dealt with in the lesson. They go deeper and may take about ten minutes every day for a week to complete. Make sure to dedicate sufficient time and space to each weekly exercise, to be able to fully experience it and experiment with it. As you read this book, I invite you to change the exercises, dismiss certain ideas, and develop others. *This is never a one-size-fit-all experience – reshape it to fit your own path.*

In addition to the exercises, each lesson illustrates a psychological measurement tool (scale or questionnaire) that enables you to test your own levels of a concept related to the topic discussed. For example, in lesson 6, which deals with the art of presence and meditation techniques, it is suggested you complete a mindfulness questionnaire, which measures the level of your mindfulness in everyday life. All the scales and questionnaires selected for this book are psychometric evaluations that have been fully tested and validated in a variety of psychological studies. It should be kept in mind that these are merely quantitative measurements, which might not match your personal experiences in full. And yet, by contemplating your scores and their meaning in relation to your own experiences, you will find it easier to make the discussion of a certain concept a personal one.

While you read the book, you may wish to keep a journal and note down the personal insights you gain through reading and practice. If you come across an idea or an advice that seems relevant and important, write a few words about it in your journal. When you are through reading the book, you will have a documented illustration of your own journey. This will make it easier to make sense of your personal conclusions and your growth process.

Lesson 1: Psychology & Spirituality

Psychology

We begin with a simple definition of psychology and spirituality that will later serve as a point of reference in the discussion of these terms. The word "psychology" comes from Greek: "psyche" is the word for "mind" or "soul", and "logos" means study. In other words, psychology is the study of the mind or the soul. Significantly, in the West psychology is only referred to as the study of the mind, whereas the "soul" part is completely ignored. Although psychology could have been the discipline that brought together the mind and the soul, the purely analytical approach adopted in the West was unable to accommodate the soul. Students reading psychology at the university often tell me that they are disappointed with their program. Many of them enrolled because they genuinely desired to better understand themselves and others, and to enhance their self-awareness and self-growth. To their disappointment, they find themselves spending long hours studying statistics and other aspects of psychology that appear to be less relevant to self-discovery. This gap between their original expectations and reality frequently causes frustration. I believe that all aspects of psychology are valuable, and that without statistics it would not be possible to conduct high-quality research; yet I am also convinced that failing to include the spiritual aspect of psychology in the curricula has put the psychology boat on a course that runs close to the essential questions of life but does not really touch upon them.

Psychology as we know it deals with the mind: the way we think, consciously form concepts, understand the world around us and make sense of it.

Spirituality

Defining spirituality is significantly harder and less clear cut, primarily because there are different approaches to spiritually, each generating a different definition. Sociologists, for example, are mostly interested in the impact of spirituality on social institutions, philosophers tend to focus on the philosophical implications of spirituality, and theologians are likely to ponder over the part of spirituality in the religious experience. In the present book, spirituality is regarded as a practical tool to achieve self-growth, because it paves the way for *transcendence*. It helps transcend the analytical functioning and cognitive processing of the mind, and makes room for other experiences. It might be easier to contemplate the spiritual experience from a psychological point of view: Psychology differentiates between cognition and meta-cognition. Cognition deals with one's thinking processes while meta-cognition is defined as "thinking about thinking". Imagine focusing your attention on an apple. You are using your cognitive faculties to become aware of the colours and aroma of the apple, but the experience rarely ends there: your meta-cognition immediately enters into action, and your mind generates thoughts in reaction to whatever is at the centre of your cognition at that moment (in this case the apple). Your meta-cognition may produce reactions such as "wow, what a beautiful apple, I should have bought more" or "I hope it has no worms in it". Spirituality points the way to transcending meta-cognition, that is, staying conscious of the apple but avoiding a parade of thoughts and reactions to it. This implies a capability to fully immerse one's awareness in the moment.

Spirituality is an invitation for a journey of transcendence that will transform your present illusionary self, the Ego Formed Self, into your Authentic Self. The discipline of spirituality regards what you perceive as your 'self' as an illusion that is an obstacle on your path to freedom. In lesson 4 we discuss the concept of self, understand the difference between the Ego Formed Self and the Authentic Self, and perform exercises that will lead you from one to the other.

In the West, an interesting shift is noticed in the way spirituality is perceived. The number of people who realise that their lives are incomplete has been growing. People understand that they have been evading certain aspects offered by life due to apprehension and discomfort. A growing feeling of oppression drives them to seek an alternative, a way to deal with these difficulties, break the boundaries and experience freedom. This is where spirituality comes in. Once they are willing to face meaningful questions, spirituality clears the way for growth. It enables them to transcend the limitations they perceive, with emphasis on "perceive". In many cases, the restrictions that exist in life stem from individual perspectives, and from people's concepts about their limits. Spirituality invites you to transcend your boundaries, and experience life with clarity and greater choice.

Spirituality has become increasingly popular because it is so relevant to our time. Look no further than the mushrooming of spiritual courses and retreats, nourished by frustration and difficulty. But the proliferation of spiritual books and courses does not necessarily guarantee quality. Many of the teachings on offer have very little to do with the spiritual essence of growth, and are merely by-products of the New Age trend. Concepts such as "let go", "live in the present", "just be" are tossed around, but their meaning remains obscure. Many individuals have been visiting spiritual workshops and retreats time and again for years, but have not succeeded in truly evolving and changing. To distinguish between an empty spiritual discussion and a meaningful one, look for their outcomes, find out whether or not change was achieved. An authentic spiritual process that touches upon essential questions about the true nature of one's consciousness is bound to produce change. Your life, your experiences, your attitude, and your understanding of your self will all change. That is your indicator as to the fact that you are engaging with genuine work that is relevant and meaningful for you. It is also crucial to emphasise the words "for you" in this context. A spiritual journey is personal; transcendence and growth are therefore achieved using subjective tools. A certain book, teacher, or workshop might be highly relevant and meaningful for one person but useless for another. Learning to recognise the tools that are relevant and meaningful for you is an important aspect of the spiritual journey.

As already mentioned psychology and spirituality must combine to bring about growth. Growing means daring to go beyond your personal boundaries. We all conduct our lives according to our personal definition of self, which carries with it a series of boundaries and limitations. Growth means pushing the boundaries to expand one's inner space. In practice, this implies that certain options, which were previously out of bounds, are now permitted and available. You have pushed your boundary, you have grown, and therefore you have the choice to say "yes" to certain things that used to be an automatic "no" in the past. This process frequently provokes two conflicting emotions: excitement and apprehension. While the adventurous prospect of going beyond your own boundaries and exploring new territories is exciting, it also provokes apprehension and anxiety. New experiences touch on the unknown, and most of us are intimidated by the unknown.

Religion vs. spirituality

The concepts of religion and spirituality are often confused, and must be clarified and told apart. Historically, the rise of secularism in the mid-1900s necessitated making a distinction between spirituality and religion. Earlier, a religious person was automatically regarded as spiritual, and vice versa. Secularism advocated disengagement from religion, and yet individuals maintained their inner spirituality, ascribing new and distinct connotations to it. Although religion and spirituality both search for that meaningful and transcendent experience referred to as "sacred", there is a thorough difference between them: Religion leans on group-validated organised means and methods, and prescribes specific practices that must be maintained within the group. It thus combines the search for the sacred with group-validated means. Spirituality, on the other hand, does not prescribe any rules, means or methods to determine the nature of its search element. By the same token, it is possible to practice religion by following group-validated means and methods without actually being spiritual, that is, without engaging in a quest for the sacred or for transcendence.

In a study[1] we conducted, my colleagues and I measured the level of spirituality in 205 participants. We evaluated their quest for the sacred, e.g., whether or not they had experienced transcendence, and their sense of oneness with the environment. We also measured the prominence of religious involvement in their lives as manifest in their adherence to group-validated means and methods (e.g., frequency of visits to a place of worship). Four categories emerged from the scores obtained for religious involvement (R) and spirituality (S) – R+S-; R-S+; R+S+; R-S- – representing four possible combinations: high religious involvement and low spirituality, low religious involvement and high spiritually, high levels of both, and low levels of both. In the same experiment, we also measured the participants' wellbeing, using as criteria the levels of meaning in life, self-actualisation (fulfilling one's potential), and willingness to undertake the exploration of self-growth. The findings were fascinating. Two groups, R+S+ and R-S+, where spirituality was prominent with or without a religious context, consistently showed higher levels of wellbeing. The group with the lowest levels of wellbeing was the R+S- one, where religious involvement was high, but spirituality levels were low. In other words, the results indicated that spirituality, especially the aspects of meaning in life, self-fulfilment, and self-growth, is a crucial constituent of wellbeing. Notably, religion was found to have the power to enhance wellbeing if it incorporates spirituality. Note that all the tested aspects of wellbeing were the products of one's own inner exploration and could only spring from the individual seeking them. Take for example the matter of meaning in life. Your sense of meaning stems from your individual journey of exploration and from the questions you ask. Meaning in life is not obtainable off the shelf, but must be conceived individually. Spirituality rises from your own creativity, courage, and personal choices, all powerful triggers of transformation.

Psychology and spirituality: The meeting point

As already explained, psychology focuses on cognitive processes such as knowledge, thoughts and ideas and on their interconnection, while spirituality is involved with experiences that transcend these processes.

Psychology and spirituality could be described as "feet on the ground, head in the sky". Psychology represents the "grounding" effect, in which the mind is used for thinking, rationalizing, and understanding life. Spirituality transcends rational thought and evolves intuitively over one's lifetime. Living a full life would mean embracing these different aspects of life, and maintaining a balance between them. Most people tend to search for a single unambiguous answer and dismiss all others. They either follow the mind-oriented psychological path or the intuitive transcendental one. Many members of the academic milieu reject vehemently all intuitive alternatives; they strongly believe that life should only be experienced through the mind. But many spiritual groups with which I am acquainted first-hand, see the mind as the enemy, and consider intuitive transcendent experiences as the only valid tools in life. By adhering to their one-sided views, both groups are restricting themselves. While being well equipped to deal with certain situations, they are ill equipped to deal with others. Rather than being contradictory, mind-based and intuitive-based experiences are complementary. They represent two aspects of the entity we call life. Certain moments in life require mind-oriented skills, while in others one must let go of the mind and act intuitively. Having both options at one's disposal at any given moment offers greater flexibility and taking action properly. This could happen only when both the psychological and the spiritual are alive within you. To realize in full the potential of growth in your life, you must be able to shift between the psychological and the spiritual poles *in accordance with the situation and at your own choice.*

Psychology and spirituality: Interdependence

Because psychology is based upon the mind, it has an important role in our journey towards self-awareness. Psychology is the means to explore and map out your mind, and understand its hidden motivations. The mind contains fragmentary information that ultimately defines who you are. Psychology helps you get in touch with this information, and gain insights on who you are and how you define your self. Spirituality, on the other hand, aims to transcend this rational processing. The newly acquired ability to transcend *that which has been acknowledged* is the point where psychology and spirituality meet. To transcend something, one must be aware that it actually exists. In other words, awareness is the key word. To become who you really are, you must transcend your illusionary perception of yourself. Since this illusion is based upon mind constructs, the awareness gained through psychological processing is necessary for spiritual transcendence. By exploring your psychological processes you get acquainted with your mind's definition of yourself. Psychology is therefore crucial to the spiritual journey for transcendence. Thus there is a strong bond between psychology and spirituality: Psychology is the means by which you get to know your mind, spirituality enables you to transcend your mind. They are essential for one another.

What stands in your way to living a full and free life: The concepts of personality and ego

One major obstacle stands in your way to living your life fully: *You are not experiencing life as it really is*. You may think this weird: "Of course I experience my life, what else would I be experiencing?" My reply is that you are actually experiencing *your personal interpretation of life*. The difference between the two is the difference between conditioning and freedom. We are rarely in touch with each and every moment of our life, and are therefore unable to connect directly and clearly to whatever comes our way. In fact, most of us bring our opinions, ideas, thoughts, and beliefs into our interpretation of each moment, drowning it. This prevents experiencing each moment as it is. Imagine the sun coming out and bathing you with its light and warmth. If you could simply bask in its warmth without further reaction, you would be experiencing life as it is. But this is almost impossible for most of us; a series of reactions immediately light up in our minds: "I wish it were this warm all the time" or "It's too hot, I should have applied sun screen". Every reaction pulls us away from the experience of life as it is, replacing it with our personal interpretation of life. We are constantly reaching out to the experience, but hardly ever manage to penetrate the many layers that wrap it.

What is the source of this personal interpretation? What is it that prevents our first-hand encounter with life? Psychologists call it *personality*. Spiritual teachers call it *ego*. What is personality? "Personality structure is described in terms of *components* that (once they are fully formed) are considered *stable and enduring*. Personality processes are descriptions of *motivational states*, which give rise to behaviour whose expression is *mediated* by that structure".[2] The first essential element of this definition is that our personality is comprised of components, many mosaic-

16

like pieces that come together to form one structure – the self. These components are quite stable and enduring. As time goes by, the components that develop within us tend to grow steadier and more solid. Individual components apply to different moments in life, becoming an integral part of our personality. Significantly, these components prompt the personality processes that determine our motivational states. The motivation that drives us towards a certain moment depends on the components that make up our personality. Whether you tend to be enthusiastic, bored, connected, disconnected, committed, or avoiding, depends on inner components that generate your motivational states. I have heard people say: "I just felt disengaged, the feeling came out of nowhere, I have no idea why I felt this way". Statements such as this indicate that the persons who utter them are blind to the way in which their personality components work. One's motivation (or lack of it) is never coincidental; it springs from a mental component and naturally gives rise to certain behaviours. The impact of a personality component does not end with motivation, but also affects one's behaviour, choices, and actions. It therefore has a very real impact on life and the way people experience it. The last part of the definition deals with mediation. The structure of our personality is a mediator that determines our behavioural expressions. In other words, the experience of a certain moment and the behaviour it entails rarely interface directly, because a personality component stands in the middle and mediates between them. This mediation results in a subjective interpretation rather than an unbiased experience of life.

From a spiritual point of view, the ego plays a similar role. The ego consists of beliefs, expectations and desires, which together weave the fabric of our experiences. Similar to personality, the ego affects our thoughts, emotions and reactions, much like a puppeteer who controls his puppets by invisible strings. The process is so natural that most of the time people are not aware that their reactions spring from a certain aspect of their ego. We frequently miss the roots of our reaction because we lack the tools required to notice the link between them. We are blind to the strings that manipulate us.

The ego may be described as the eye through which the mind perceives reality. When you approach a certain moment, you do not see it as it truly is because your sense of seeing passes through the filter of the ego. Imagine the ego as a pair of sunglasses that change colour in different situations. Much of our growth journey is about realizing that we wear these glasses, and developing the option of taking them off when we choose to.

It is easy to notice that the concepts of personality and ego have very similar foundations. They both deal with the constructs of what we consider as our self. Although different lexical terms are used, their meaning is remarkably similar. While I was studying psychology and spirituality, I noticed that they have many points in common, raise similar questions, and often interweave, in spite of their different titles.

Here and now exercise 1: Naming your ego concepts

In your journal, describe one central ego concept for important domains of your life, such as romantic relations, work, family, friends, and leisure. Look for a different ego concept in each domain. In your search, try to recall your expectations from people, your needs or fears, your insights about yourself, and your beliefs concerning that domain – any of those would be an example for an ego concept.

Why must a personality/ego be created?

How would you feel if you had no clear understanding of who you are or of what you like and dislike? Most of us would feel extremely confused. Our personal insights about life and about ourselves are a safety net that keeps us protected from a reality that would have otherwise been confusing. Because we are uncomfortable with the unknown, we strive to make reality as understandable as possible by gathering knowledge about the world through our experience, and transforming it into what we perceive as "objective" truths: This is the way to react in certain circumstances, I like this but not that, I fancy this person and not that one... Of course, this list represents the components of our ego or our personality, and creates a sense of stability and familiarity in a world that would have otherwise been perceived as chaotic. Coming to realize that I should avoid sharing my feelings with my colleagues because they were not discrete in the past would give me better control over the process of selecting my friends, as I have personal guidelines to follow. Although this may come at the price of restricting my choices, the fact remains that this makes my life easier, more stable and predictable. Here is the rationale of the matter:

We struggle to feel safe and secure, because we fear the unknown.

We are intimately familiar with our character traits and self-concepts. Because they are durable and steady, they reduce our concern about the unknown.

We are able to predict our responses to different situations. This means that there is less of the unknown in our lives.

If life is more predictable and seems safer, we are not as anxious and uncomfortable.

This rationalization explains our need for ego concepts. With each ego concept that is formed in our minds we feel that our experience of the world becomes more controllable. They are part of our pursuit of a safe and secure life. They are the antidote to what we perceive as a stressful existence, where anything can happen at any moment.

Psychological measurement 1: Personal Need for Structure questionnaire

The Personal Need for Structure questionnaire3 was developed to assess your need for structure and your responses to lack of structure. This measurement is highly relevant in the context of our pursuit of a safe and secure life which invites the formation of ego concepts.

Instructions: Read each of the following statements and decide how much you agree with each according to your attitudes, beliefs and experiences. It is important for you to realise that there are no 'right' or 'wrong' answers to these questions. People are different, and we are interested in how you feel. Please respond according to the following 6-point scale:

1	Strongly disagree
2	Moderately disagree
3	Slightly disagree
4	Slightly agree
5	Moderately agree
6	Strongly agree

1	It upsets me to go into a situation without knowing what I can expect from it.	
2	I'm not bothered by things that interrupt my daily routine.	
3	I enjoy having a clear and structured mode of life.	
4	I like to have a place for everything and everything in its place.	
5	I enjoy being spontaneous.	
6	I find that a well-ordered life with regular hours makes my life tedious.	
7	I don't like situations that are uncertain.	
8	I hate to change my plans at the last minute.	
9	I hate to be with people who are unpredictable.	
10	I find a routine enables me to enjoy life more.	
11	I enjoy the exhilaration of being in unpredictable situations	
12	I become uncomfortable when the rules in a situation are not clear	

Scoring: Final scores are obtained by reversing the scores (1=6,

6=1, 2=5, 5=2, 3=4, 4=3) of items 2, 5, 6, and 11 and summing up the scores of all 12 items. Your score is the arithmetic mean of the 12 items. Higher scores stand for higher need for structure. The mean score obtained in experimental studies was 3.1.

During the spiritual journey you are about to take you will be faced with the challenge of giving up your ego concepts, those preconceptions that are supposedly protecting you from the chaos of life and its stress and anxiety. The importance of spiritual growth, and the meaningful transformation that occurs once you let go of the concepts you have accumulated, are discussed time and again in this book. Abandoning these concepts is not easy. In fact, the experience will probably be frightening. You will become vulnerable because you will surrender part of your defences and allow yourself to experience life with sincerity and courage.

We often create ego concepts in response to difficulty, when we feel vulnerable in the face of a challenge, and seek to regain our sense of safety and control. For example, you could develop the ego concept "I shouldn't let anyone in" following a break up with a romantic partner in response to your vulnerability and hurt. Although an ego concept such as this is psychologically relevant for a limited period of recuperation, you have very little control over its growth. It could grow roots and become an internal motivator that shapes your conscious or unconscious choices and behaviours. It is a defence mechanism that was initially useful in the face of difficulty but has been "defending" you since against a nonexistent foe. Once you form an ego concept, it quickly disengages itself from the particular event with which it was once linked and becomes an internal rule. Your psychological journey is a walk down the path of your personal defence mechanisms, during which you realize that many of them should have been discarded, but formed instead another layer that stands between you and actual reality.

Defence mechanisms and the longing for safety and stability are not the only reasons for creating and accumulating self-concepts. We also do this to minimize our cognitive effort. A cognitive effort is the effort your mind is required to invest in processing under different circumstances. A brand new situation would reasonably involve a greater cognitive effort, because it calls for grasping and assessing the situation and the people involved. If a series of pre-existent assumptions are at your disposal when you approach a new situation, you can save much of this cognitive effort. You already "know" how to behave, what to say, what the people around you will do. Many shortcuts of this kind simplify your interaction with the world, making it unnecessary to actually be present in the moment and act appropriately. Pre-contemplated actions and behaviours make it possible to minimize the cognitive effort required in life. In lesson 3, we discuss aware vs. unaware thinking, and the circumstances in which aware thinking generates a productive cognitive shortcut, while unaware thinking leads to cognitive shortcuts that block the way to freedom.

An idea of your self

In search for safety, people focus their identity on an *idea* of their self, i.e. on the mental abstraction called Ego or Personality. All the information concerning one's self and the world can be defined in terms of aware or unaware assumptions, or ego concepts, that colour one's personal experience, for example:

- I am not creative, I have no imagination
- I am an intelligent person
- I can never do what I want to do
- I am very sensitive / insensitive

Or as beliefs about the world, such as:

- There is something wrong about money
- Performing arts are a profession that will take me nowhere

Note that positive and negative assumptions are both part of our self. On a psychological level, it would be more beneficial to adhere to positive assumptions about our self than to negative ones. For example, your self-confidence and self-esteem would gain more if you adopted ego concepts such as "smart" and "successful" and not "boring" or "stupid". Such ego concepts would make you more resilient psychologically. However, from a spiritual perspective this is not the case. From the spiritual point of view, any such assumption about your self would be perceived as being part of the illusion that stands in your way to life as it is. Be it a positive or a negative assumption, it would still colour your glasses and somehow distort the experience of the moment. From a spiritual point of view, freedom would only be achieved if we had the choice of taking off the glasses, and removing the concepts that colour reality with positive or negative assumptions.

Jane Roberts invites us to imagine the ego as a fence through which we see the world. We make an effort to capture as much as possible, but our vision is limited to the cracks and spaces between the poles: "You must first recognize the existence of such barriers, you must see them or you will not even realize that you are not free, simply because you will not see beyond the fences; they will represent the boundaries of your experience".[4]

This quotation illustrates the role psychology plays in the spiritual journey. Roberts advises us to first recognize the ego concepts that are floating around in our minds. Those assumptions you make about your self, about other people, and about the world around you. If you do not recognize these assumptions and the impact they have on your relationship with life, you will not be aware of the fact that you are not free.

You are free to experience the adventures that life is offering you only as far as your personal "fences", your ego concepts, allow you. As long as you do not recognize the fences and their influence you would not be able to realize how limited your experience is. Although your ability to experience life "as it is" could be unlimited, your interpretation of the experience stands in the way, and restricts this original potential. Remember that these assumptions, your personal "fences", are all mental concepts, that is, part of your own psychological experience. In the course of the psychological journey you will discover your mind and its assumptions. This journey is essential to the spiritual transcendence that enables you to pull down the "fences" and experience life as it is. Transcendence, in this context, means bypassing mind processes, and relating to life directly, free of assumptions. To achieve transcendence it would be necessary to undergo the psychological process by which you get intimately acquainted with your mind's patterns.

I have heard students say that their life has lost its sense of adventure, the feeling that anything is possible. This could be the result of accumulated ego concepts. With time, the list of assumptions grows longer, curbing our experiences. The potentials of life disappear and experiences that had the sense of an adventure (as all potentials were incorporated within them) now seem to be dull and grey. Why this change? The experience that had been so exciting a few years earlier has not changed; it is your own perspective, the accumulation of ego concepts that had such a detrimental effect on your sense of vitality and adventure. Perhaps the best way to illustrate this process is to take a look at children. For a child, every stimulus is a celebration; every moment is an invitation for an adventure. Children do not have as many expectations, fears, desires and assumptions as adults, and are therefore able to simply enjoy the moment. Children sense intuitively that there are no bounds to their experiences, and they celebrate this freedom. You may recall that unrestrained sense of liberty, and long to recapture it. In many ways, regaining that child-like attitude is the essence of the spiritual journey. I don't suggest that you become irresponsible as most young children are, but that you revive that sense of awe and joy that you have lost over the years. This child-like experience has been stifled by ego concepts. Transcending these assumptions and ideas could take us back to that original, free space.

Weekly exercise 1: Discovering your ego concepts

Use the table below to fill in the required information. For each of the areas listed in the left column of the table, find three ego concepts of your own. You may wish to select them out of the various assumptions, desires, fears, needs, ideas, beliefs, or expectations that you have with regard to these areas of life. For example, in the romantic relationship box you may decide to write "my partner must invest in the relationship as much as I do" or "my partner should always be patient with me" or "in good relationships presents are frequently exchanged". In the work box you may decide to write "my only reason for working is the salary I am paid" or "my job is boring" or "I wish I could work in a different place or with different people".

	Three ego concepts that produce an interpretation of the experience	An experience which has been interpreted by an ego concept
Romantic relationship		
Work		
Friends		
Family		
Leisure		

Beginning today, examine your inner self every day for a week, and note down events, experiences, and situations during which you noticed an ego concept affecting your behaviour and reaction. Note down as many events as you can. For example, if you have the ego concept "my job is boring" you could note down a moment when you chose not to engage in a certain task because you "knew" that your job was boring, and that made you evade responsibility. This part of the exercise is meant to call your awareness to various experiences as they happen, and to make you recognise *the root* of your behaviour. The ego concepts that you noted down in the first box are not idle in your mind. They take active part in many situations related to that area of life. This exercise invites you to recognise the influence of an ego concept and the way it manipulates your behaviour.

People tell that the Buddha used to give a weekly talk. After attending one of these talks, a man approached the Buddha and told him that he was very disappointed. "What is it that disappoints you"? asked the Buddha. The man replied that he had been attending the weekly talks regularly for three years. He saw many of his fellow students find deeper peace and contentment, but his own mind was still as chaotic and troubled as it had been. The Buddha then asked him whether he joined his daily meditation sessions, and the man said that he was unable to because he had other obligations. The Buddha asked him, unexpectedly, whether he was a citizen of that town. "No," replied the man, "I come from the city of Amritsar". The Buddha then asked: "Has any of your friends ever asked you for directions to travel to Amritsar?" The man replied that many people have, because Amritsar is a holy city they wished to visit. "Have all of these friends visited and toured Amritsar"? The Buddha asked. "Of course not", said the man, "some of them were merely planning the journey or hoping to make it one day". The Buddha looked at the man with a compassionate smile and said "A teacher can only offer instruction; the student must be the one to take the walk. If you wish to see Amritsar you must set out on a journey that will take you there; if you wish to reach peace, you must venture the journey towards it. By attending my weekly sessions you have acquired an important tool that shows you the right direction, but you must start walking all the same".

This book will help you draw a map, but detailed and clear as the map may be, it will remain nothing but a piece of paper, unless you actually walk the path it traces, that is, actually practice. By carrying out the weekly exercise of this lesson you will be transforming your theoretical understanding of your ego concepts into an intimate experience and knowledge of their influence.

Lesson 2: The Meditative Skill

In the previous lesson we discussed the psychological process of discovering the ego concepts that you carry in your mind. We are now shifting our attention to spirituality, to gain a deeper understanding of the transcendence concept it incorporates. What exactly are we transcending? How is transcendence achieved? Why is transcendence so relevant to our spiritual journey? These are crucial questions that will be answered as we explore a topic considered the essence of spiritual work: Meditation.

The influence of meditation

Over the past three decades, a radical and extremely interesting change has occurred in the way people in the West regard meditation. Until the 1980s, the term "meditator" brought to mind a guy in an orange robe, with a long, white, messy beard, sitting alone on top of a mountain. Nowadays, future mothers engage in pregnancy meditation, stressed bank employees meditate to relax, athletes meditate to improve their performance, and people undergoing therapy meditate to improve their condition. Meditation is suddenly thought to be cool. There are several reasons for this significant change. Two of the most important ones are therapy and scientific research. Nowadays, different branches of psychological therapy use meditation as a central tool for working with clients. Counselling psychologists, psychotherapists and clinical psychologists all utilise the power of meditation and integrate it into the therapeutic process aimed to resolve a variety of difficulties faced by the clients. Clinical psychologists frequently offer their clients meditation sessions and recommend that they practice meditation daily. Meditation is also included in Cognitive Behavioural Therapy (CBT), one of the most commonly used models of therapy, whose purpose is changing people's behaviour by changing their thought patterns.

Meditation has become so popular in CBT that a new branch was developed – MBCT (Mindfulness Based Cognitive Therapy). MBCT combines traditional CBT strategies with the experience of Mindfulness, and has proved very effective in treating various conditions, especially depression. But why has meditation become so prominent in therapy all of a sudden? The answer lies in scientific research. Western society expects each of its products to be scientifically tested in a laboratory before it passes the legitimacy test. Meditation went through thousands of experiments with astonishing results. Even the greatest believers in meditation are frequently surprised at the potency and efficiency of the meditative experience. Meditation has a powerfully favourable impact in different spheres.[6] Physiologically, meditation has been shown to:

- Have a positive effect on the cardiovascular system by lowering heartbeat rate and blood pressure
- Assist in controlling hypertension
- Assist in effectively treating certain conditions (e.g., diabetes)
- Relieve pain

On a psychological or cognitive level, meditation has been shown to:

- Improve reaction time and perceptual motor skills
- Enhance de-automatisation by breaking the habit of acting automatically without full attention
- Improve concentration and attention
- Help overcome addiction and chemical dependency
- Improve memory
- Decrease anxiety and stress
- Improve sleep

The subjective reports of people who engage in meditation describe the following influences of meditation:

- Equanimity
- Inner peace
- Bliss
- Clearer perception
- Energy
- Excitement

I invite you to re-read this list and imagine that someone is offering you a new vitamin – Vitamin M. You are told to take it once a day and then rest for ten minutes. To promote the distribution of this new vitamin, it is offered to you for free. In your opinion, what would happen at the pharmacies? I would imagine long queues, dozens of people fighting for the privilege of getting hold of the amazing new vitamin M. Now consider this: This vitamin is already at your disposal, cost free, with results that have been proven by numerous scientific studies.

Meditation is also very helpful in dealing with addictions. It increases our ability to control our attention (see below) and shift it away from nagging addictive stimuli (cigarettes, food, etc.) to the present moment (a conversation with a friend, or reading, for example), thus significantly reducing dependency. In a study conducted at Yale University,[5] a group of nicotine-dependent adults was randomly given one of two treatments: mindfulness meditation, and the American Lung Association's standard treatment to quit smoking. Both treatments were administered over four weeks. In terms of reducing cigarette use, the results of the mindfulness group were better than those of the group that was given the standard treatment and, no less important, the first group had more success in maintaining this change four months after the treatment. In average, the mindfulness participants reduced their cigarette consumption by 90% (from eighteen to two cigarettes per day); 35% of them quit smoking altogether.

Meditation has also been linked with the treatment of stress, anxiety, and depression. One main reason for these complaints has to do with our mind's tendency to plunge uncontrollably into negative thoughts that are usually rooted in the past. To prevent this from happening, it is tremendously helpful to learn how to calm down the mind and focus on the present moment. Several meta-analyses[6,7] (combining the results of dozens of different studies) support this argument. Sleep disorder, for example, is a complaint meditation has been shown to be very helpful with. In the US and the UK, approximately one in four individuals suffers from a sleep disorder. Meditation reduces anxiety and stress, and the relaxation it brings improves the quality of our sleep.

The effect of meditation is not limited to difficult experiences; meditation also helps boost our wellbeing. There is a strong connection between the experience of meditation and positive psychology, i.e., the study of human strengths and best potentials. One of the goals of meditation, indeed one of its consequences as well, is to catalyse the development of our internal potentials and improve wellbeing. Meditation is linked with higher level factors such as self-esteem, self-actualisation, autonomy, satisfaction with life, and positive affect.[8] Research has also indicated that dedicated meditators experience significantly higher levels of psychological wellbeing than non-meditators. Meditation has also been shown to promote positive inter-personal emotions such as empathy and compassion, while improving self-acceptance, meaning and purpose in life, and personal growth.[9]

Perhaps the most amazing discovery of research is that meditation changes the physical structure of the brain. Compared with non-meditators, the brains of individuals who meditate regularly have specific regions that are more developed. These are the regions associated, for example, with attention, interoception (sensitivity to stimuli coming from within the body), and sensory processing.[10] Meditation has been shown to have an effect on an area called the Amygdala, located at the base of the brain, which participates in processing emotions. People who meditate show weaker activation of the Amygdala, which results in greater emotional stability and an improved response to stress.[11]

No matter which of these positive influences you are seeking when you turn to meditation, you will benefit from an array of wonderful influences as long as you truly meditate (as opposed to drowsing or daydreaming). Having understood the benefits of meditation, we are now going to understand its precise meaning. How is it defined, and how does it work?

Different kinds of meditation

We often discuss meditation as if it were a single experience; in fact, there are hundreds of different meditation techniques. The variety of techniques that lie under the umbrella of meditation is vast. One meditation teacher may ask you to focus on your sense organs, while the other will tell you to completely avert your attention from your senses, and in both cases you will be meditating. In one workshop you may be asked to visualise certain images, while in another you will be forbidden to pay attention to any kind of imagery, and yet in both cases you will be meditating. In one class you may sit rigidly, completely immobile, while in another you may walk or dance, and these are both meditation techniques. You could be encouraged to allow feelings and emotions or you might be asked to disregard any emotional response, and still be meditating in both cases. How is this possible? How can such fundamentally different experiences all have the title "meditation"? What do they all have in common?

Defining meditation

One simple and accurate definition of meditation states:

"Meditation refers to a *family of techniques* which have in common a *conscious attempt* to *focus attention* in a *non-analytical way* and an attempt not to dwell on discursive, ruminating thought".[12] According to this definition, meditation is "a family of techniques", a variety of different experiences that are all meditative in nature. What they all have in common is a "conscious attempt to focus your attention". You must consciously choose to point your attention at a particular object, and keep it there. Another important point is that this should be done in a "non-analytical way", in other words, without cognitive reaction to the focus of attention. The kind of attention you must apply here is unique. We are all "addicted" to mental reactions. They happen unconsciously. You see a flower and your mind immediately kicks off into reaction mode: "Wow, this is the prettiest flower I have seen this spring", which may lead to "I should get one for my partner", and then "she will then forgive me for yesterday's fight", and "I shouldn't have said what I said". And the flower? Long out of your awareness. The focus of your attention has wandered off in a chain-reaction of thought that pulled you away from the moment, the flower. As stated in this definition, meditation means focusing your attention on something and pulling it away from your ruminating thoughts; your attention remains fully focused on the point you have chosen.

Here and now exercise 2: The wandering mind

To illustrate the matter of the focal point I would like you to choose an object in your immediate environment, such as a cup of coffee, a chair, or a vase. Now, point your full attention at this object, while closely observing your mind. Try to focus your attention on that object for as long as you can. How much time had passed before your mind wandered? Repeat the exercise with a couple of different objects (different focal points) and observe the length of time that passes before your mind begins wandering. You may find yourself thinking about the object you chose, about the exercise, about work you must do later – your thoughts will pull your awareness away from the focal point.

Who is in charge of your awareness?

I have run this little exercise in class with many students, and found that the average time after which people report that their mind has wandered is roughly a few seconds. In certain cases attention shifts away from the object instantaneously, while in others this may take a few seconds; I have rarely heard anyone mention a longer time. Now, what exactly is the meaning of this? You were asked to direct your full attention at a certain object. You made a conscious effort to keep your attention focused on it. And yet, after no more than a few seconds, the focus is gone, and you are chasing after other thoughts, objects, or ideas. I therefore ask you: Who is in charge of your awareness? Please, give this important question real thought. This is not a philosophical question; it is nothing but practical, and has an enormous influence on the quality of your life. How many times have you decided to do something only to find yourself, hours later, doing something else, your original plan completely neglected? This is a direct result of your lack of control over your attention; your awareness has a life of its own, and fluctuation seems to be one of its inevitable characteristics. Fortunately, it is not really inevitable. Meditation actually enables you to take charge of your awareness, and develop the capacity to choose (yet again, choice is freedom) the focus of your attention at any given moment.

Psychological studies fully support the concept that meditation changes the quality of your attention. In a large-scale study[13] conducted in Colorado, a group of 30 meditators joined a 3-month meditation retreat where they meditated for five hours daily. During their stay in the retreat, the participants were asked three times to complete computer tasks that measured their ability to make fine visual distinctions and sustain visual attention. The participants' performances kept improving: Each time they had better results in making the visual distinctions, and their attention was enhanced. What is more, they also improved their ability to sustain their attention, and were able to keep their enhanced perception for a longer period of time. In other words, with time, it became easier for the participants to sustain attention voluntarily, to focus on a particular focal point for longer periods of time. Participants, who were re-tested five months after the retreat, were found to have kept this enhanced attention, particularly if they continued meditating daily. These results touch on the spiritual perspective of meditation and self-growth discussed in the previous paragraph. They support yet again the spiritual idea described long ago (in Buddhist scripts, for example), that meditation enhances the span of attention, which is now being substantiated scientifically by psychological tools.

We now realise that all meditation techniques share one practice: focusing your attention in a non-analytical way. Whether you are sitting with your eyes closed, jumping up and down, taking a walk in nature, or visualising a certain image, you are engaging in meditation once your awareness is focused on a particular object (breath/body/image) in a particular way (non-analytic).

If you are washing the dishes, just wash the dishes

Further contemplation of the descriptions given above would lead us to the conclusion that *any* moment in which we are one with the experience may be defined as meditation. Once you make a conscious effort to focus your attention in a non-analytical way, any experience is an invitation for meditation: jogging and focusing your attention on the movement of your muscles, washing the dishes and focusing your attention on the feeling of water on your skin, or combining both by swimming and keeping your attention focused on your body as it cuts through the water. The nature of the activity does not matter; what matters is the quality of your consciousness (focused and non-analytical). Remember, if you think about past or future events while you jog, wash the dishes or swim – you are not meditating, because your mind is processing thoughts that are pulling you away from the experience itself. A wandering mind is an essential factor in breaking "oneness", the idea of being one with the moment. Whenever you direct your attention at a certain activity without analysing it you become one with it. Every bit of your attention is focused on that object and you become united, on an experiential level, with whatever it is that you are doing. This is a union of your awareness and the activity. This union is lost when your mind interferes by reacting; your awareness is then pulled away from the activity itself to thinking about it. Thinking about something does not mean being with it. Being and thinking are fundamentally different. Being only means experiencing the moment, without thinking. If the moment is an invitation to dance, and you move your body freely, all you are is that flow of movement that does not have to make any sense as it is free and natural. That is when you are one with the moment, with the activity. Your awareness and the activity are united. You *are* the dance, and nothing else exists. But if your mind interferes with the dance, it pulls your awareness away from the experience and breaks the union. You are no longer one with the dance; you are thinking *about* the dance rather than meditating.

Exactly what is the meaning of being one with the moment? This means that you are completely one with whatever you do – when you wash the dishes, for example, *all you do is wash the dishes* – you do not think about, wish for, dream of, or remember anything else. Many of us spend most of our time without being one with our experiences. We sit for a cup of tea and think about the report we must write, we sit down to write the report and picture the dishes that have to be washed, we wash the dishes and think over the conversation we are going to have with a friend, we talk with our friend and dream of having a quiet cup of tea. This is absurd: the moments constantly invite us to experience them for what they are, and we seem to consistently reject the invitation and wander elsewhere. What really happens is that we get lost in our own mind. Letting go of the chain of thoughts that follow the activity, and simply focusing our attention and diving into the experience opens an alternative way of being, the meditative one. When this happens, meditation enables transcending additional thought processes. The meditative experience is the gate into the spiritual transcendence that we discussed in lesson 1. It enables moving beyond our thoughts, ideas, and ego concepts.

Meditative technique vs. meditative state

There is a difference between a meditative *state* and a meditative *technique*. A meditative technique involves certain conscious efforts – concentration, observation, and focus of attention, all in a non-analytical way. This technique is the vehicle, the gateway. It facilitates entering a meditative state. The meditative state itself means transcending reactive thoughts. It is not a state you can consciously choose to move into. But you can choose to practice the technique, and by doing this, move towards the meditative state. In lesson 6 we explore further this meditative, transcendent state. At this point, you may imagine that it is your default state once you are able to consciously move away from the hubbub of the mind into the moment as it is. This transcendent experience is always waiting there, beyond the cognitive processing of the mind. It is an invitation that life extends to you again and again, with every breath you take. When your awareness lets go of the clatter in your mind, transcendence automatically takes over that space. That is why thinking about transcendence or wishing for it will not take you there. It will rather mean that another ego concept was translated into thought, only to pull you farther away from transcendence. All you really have to do is practice the meditative technique and it will pull you away from the non-transcendent state; your consciousness will then connect naturally to the meditative state, the transcendent experience of being.

Breathing meditation

Breathing meditation is one of the most basic and popular meditation techniques. To understand why, we should recall the fundamental reasoning underlying the meditative experience: retraining your attention. Now, consider breathing; breathing is among the few things we do all the time, day and night. No matter what activity we engage in, whether we are awake or asleep, content or dissatisfied – breathing is always there, synonymous with life. Therefore, if we wish to retrain our attention and keep it focused, taming our breathing appears to be the perfect solution. It is an anchor we can count on. All you need is to muster sufficient awareness and focus on your breathing, and you will always have an anchor to keep you in the moment. Your mind wanders, tells you stories, pulls you away from the experience? Return to your breath.

An old Zen story tells about a farmer who lives in a small house with his family, and has large fields to work. The man finds it very hard to deal with all of his obligations, and he goes to the wise man of the village for help. The wise man listens to his complaints and promises that when the farmer gets back home he will have a servant waiting to fill his orders. The farmer thanks the wise man and goes home. At home, a servant runs towards him shouting "oh master, what shall I do"? The farmer is delighted. He tells the servant to clean the house, plough the fields, and do other chores. A few weeks later, the farmer returns to the wise man and tells him that the servant is driving him crazy, demanding more work than he has to give him. "I do not have a minute of peace," complains the farmer. With a smile the wise man advises him to build a tall pole in his backyard. "Whenever the servant asks for work and there is none, tell him to climb up and down the wooden pole until you call for him".

Your own wooden pole is your breath. It is there, in the "backyard" of your consciousness, constantly ready for use as a focal point by your mind, the servant, until it is needed somewhere else. As you keep practicing the breathing meditation, your fluctuating attention learns how to return to the focal point of your choice (your breathing) and thereby control your awareness.

Understanding meditation

Before you begin your breathing meditation practice, I would like to address a number of questions and difficulties frequently experienced by both novice and experienced meditators. Getting acquainted with the items on this list may help you deal with similar challenges in your own practice.

- **Noise and Quiet:** When you begin your meditation practice, every noise is bound to be disruptive. Make sure to meditate in an environment that is as peaceful as possible. Unplug your landline and put your mobile phone on 'silent'. Find the quietest room in your home. If meditating at home is not practicable, try a local library instead. Once you become more experienced, you will find it easier to practice in a noisy location without being distracted.
- **Posture:** You may have seen others meditating crossed legged or in a lotus position. Their main purpose is to keep their back straight, so as to ensure that their posture facilitates meditation, keeping them comfortable but alert. Any posture that keeps you comfortable yet awake and alert is good. Lying down is not recommended because you might

easily fall asleep. Sitting on a chair with your back straight and slightly away from the back rest is perfectly fine. As we frequently meditate sitting down, it may be easy to remember the acronym ASS: Alert, Soft, and Sustainable. During meditation the body has to be alert, so that you remain awake, but at the same time it has to be soft, to avoid tension. Finally, as meditation may go on for a long time, the posture has to be sustainable; choosing a difficult posture, one that is impossible to remain in, would be counter-productive as you would have to move and shift frequently, and therefore break the meditative state. Maintaining an alert, soft and sustainable posture would allow a strong foundation on which you can build your meditation practice.

- **Alarm clock:** The first times you practice meditation, I advise you to use an alarm clock. During meditation the sense of time is frequently distorted. If your day has been challenging and many thoughts are pulling you away from your breathing, a couple of minutes may seem like half an hour; in a quiet day, when your mind is quite at peace, you may experience deep meditation and half an hour could seem like a couple of minutes. An alarm clock prevents constant thoughts about time – "Surely ten minutes have passed by now..." – that will make you open your eyes to peek at the time. By using an alarm clock, at least in the first few months of your practice, you would be able to let go of the issue of time and focus on your breathing.

- **When:** Students frequently ask me what the best time is to meditate. I recommend experimenting with different times to see which one is best for you. Meditation in the morning opens your day in a deeply relaxed state of mind that could linger over your day and transform it. In the evening, meditation usually follows a day of activity and accumulated stress, and could ease some of this tension and allow a calmer evening and better quality of sleep. Ideally, you could practice both in the morning and in the evening, but choosing a single time-slot that feels more natural and easy is beneficial as well.

- **Falling asleep:** At times, you may fall asleep during meditation. This is natural, but if it happens too often you might wish to consider the following: Try not to meditate on a full stomach as this may make you drowsy. Meditating on an empty stomach (or after a very light meal) is more productive. Also, make sure you are not too tired; if you practice late at night after a full day of activity, you will probably fall asleep in no time. If you meditate very early in the morning after just a few hours of sleep you may also be prone to falling asleep. This point is even more relevant if you meditate lying down. Most of the times you start to fall asleep you will find that you have allowed your head and spine to slump slightly. If you are tired and feel that you are about to fall asleep, you could breathe deeply, with an accompanying gentle sound, to make it easier to focus on breathing and remain awake and alert. You could also keep your eyes open or half open while you practice. Fully closed eyes block many environmental stimuli and make meditation easier, but this may also make you fall asleep. Most importantly, be determined to continue the meditative experience if you wish to remain awake. Remember that falling asleep is often a natural part of the meditation experience. You should consider the points mentioned above only if you discover that falling asleep has become a pattern.
- **Making time:** The issue of time management is brought up frequently by students struggling to meditate regularly. Analyse your daily schedule, and find out which of your activities can be slightly cut short to allow for the 20 minutes required for meditation every day. If possible,

avoid cutting down on your sleeping time; being tired does not enhance meditation. Try creative solutions. For example, you may be spending some time every day in public transportation or in waiting rooms. When you have gathered enough experience with meditation, and are no longer distracted by noise, meditating in these places is an optional solution. In terms of time, meditation is an excellent long-term investment. At the moment, lack of control over your mind negatively affects your productivity. In average, you may be able to remain focused on a certain task for about 40% of the time. Meditation teaches you how to "squeeze the lemon" more effectively. As you keep practicing, you will discover that the earlier 40% of productive time gradually grows and becomes 50% and then 60%. In other words, at the moment you are investing time in doing something that is going to revolutionise the way you experience time and teach you how to use it more effectively.

- **Regular practice:** As is the case with many other new experiences, you will probably be excited when you begin to practice meditation. This excitement will help you practice; but what can you do to keep practicing regularly? My students often tell me that they managed to meditate for a few weeks, and then meditation was "somehow" pushed aside and the daily practice was cut down to twice a week, then once a week, and then was completely neglected. I ask those students one simple question: Do you brush your teeth twice daily, every single day? Once you ask yourself whether or not you should meditate on a certain day, you will probably find a reason why you cannot. There is always some other important thing to do. It is all a question of priorities. You don't ask yourself every day whether you should brush your teeth or not. You internalised long ago that brushing your teeth was important, and have been doing it regularly since. Try to apply the same attitude to meditation, because meditation looks after your mind just as brushing your teeth looks after your teeth. Here is the most useful advice I can offer to ensure that your practice is stable and consistent: *Create a daily ceremony.* Choose a convenient time, plan your own setup (perhaps sitting down to meditate, or combining meditation with certain yoga postures, chanting, lighting a candle, burning some incense, anything you feel is right), and follow this routine regularly. Of course, you can eventually make any changes that come to your mind, but this initial structuring will help you get in the habit of practicing regularly. This consistent practice is the key to the growth of your meditative experience. Although it is only natural to miss a meditation session here and there, your practice must be regular and consistent if you wish to lay the foundation for awareness which, for its part, will assist you in dealing with your deeply-rooted conditioning.

Weekly exercise 2: Breathing meditation

Practice the breathing meditating 10 minutes daily for a week. If you feel comfortable with the 10-minute session you can gradually extend the practice session by 5 minutes each time or add another session on that day.

- Sit comfortably.
- Close your mouth and breathe as much as possible through your nose (It is easier to concentrate on breathing this way).
- Close your eyes (fewer stimuli to distract your mind).
- Bring your full attention to your breathing.
- Track the air entering your body: Feel it in your nostrils, and filling your lungs. Feel your chest and belly

expanding. Do the same when the air goes out of your body: your belly and chest contract, the air leaves your lungs and flows out through your nostrils.

At a certain point, you may discover that your awareness is no longer focused on your breathing. It has wandered and is now focused on another thought or image. If this happens, immediately bring your awareness back to your breathing, with a smiling attitude.

As you focus on your breath, imagine that it is a vehicle your awareness is riding. You may try to notice the sensation of the point at which your breath meets your body. The way the air touches the edges of your nostrils as it enters your nose, the feeling of the air touching the inner side of your nose and travelling into your body, the sensation of your lungs filling slowly, the different temperature of the air when it enters your body (quite cold) and when it leaves it (much warmer). The idea is to find as many sensations as possible that anchor you to your breath, to help you keep your awareness fully focused on your breath. And yet, your mind will tend to stray away from your breath and go to other thoughts. These thoughts may have to do with meditation: "why am I doing this?" or "this is boring" or "I feel much more relaxed", but they may also be entirely disconnected from meditation: "should I eat pizza tonight?" or "I feel like watching an episode of Grey's Anatomy". Not only will your mind wander, these thoughts will also invite new ones by association. The thought about pizza, for example, may make you wonder whether or not you have the ingredients in your fridge; this can lead you to think about the opening hours of the supermarket, and you may ask yourself whether you can make it on time. Our cognitive processing tends to snowball. It begins with a simple idea and quickly evolves into a complex story. Therefore, you must be quick about harnessing your attention immediately as it begins moving away from your breathing. If you don't, next thing you know, your mind has wandered. When you realise you must do something to bring your attention back to your breath, make sure to remember two important principles:

1   Act *immediately* as you observe the fluctuation. Any time gap between this realisation and re-directing the focus of your attention to your breathing will be filled with mental noise. Your mind will react to the realisation that it has wandered by producing thoughts such as "why can't I do it?" or "I wish I could stay with the breath". This is another way of the mind to sneak into the moment through the back door. To avoid this you must practice bringing your awareness immediately back to your breath.

2   When you notice that your mind has wandered, just keep smiling and remain calm. It is easy to become frustrated when you begin practicing meditation. Your mind keeps wandering, you are now becoming aware of it, you try to stop your mind wandering but it disobeys you. You may become angry or frustrated for not being able to follow the instructions. Behind this reaction is a new ego concept telling you how you are expected to perform when you meditate. To deal with this potential issue you must cultivate a compassionate attitude towards the entire experience, an attitude that accepts whatever happens instead of introducing anger and frustration into the experience. You should know that this fluctuation is completely natural. This is the way your mind has been conditioned to work for many years; congratulate yourself for finally beginning to acknowledge the true nature of your mind and for consciously trying to control it.

Meditation: Retraining your attention

What you actually do when you meditate is *retrain* your attention. For years your attention has been conditioned to fluctuate; this is the way it has learned to relate to life, each momentary focus of attention immediately leading to another. Your attention has been trained to leap quickly from one stimulus to another, without pausing to embrace any of them peacefully. Meditation slowly breaks this habit; it retrains your mind and offers you the option of calmly directing your awareness at a focal point of your choice. As you do this, your attention may wander off. This is the habitual reaction of your mind. By meditating, you break this pattern, pulling your awareness back to the chosen focal point. This is the meaning of retraining. Your attention, which used to be fluctuating and reactive, now becomes still and observing. Your mind is used to fluctuating freely but during meditation you are teaching it a new way of being. In the course of a single meditation session your mind may fluctuate many times, but you will consciously choose to bring it back to the focal point. Every success you have in doing this will gradually improve your meditative skills. Every time you pull your mind back to the focal point you will gain some additional control over it. If you wish to read faster, ride a bike, or have a better memory, all you should do is retrain your mind; focus on certain activities for a certain period of time, in a way that will improve your skills. The same applies to meditation. Consistent repetition of the meditative experience will teach you the incredible skill of always keeping your attention where you *choose* it to be. After practicing regularly this way, you will have a different answer to the question "who is in charge of your awareness?" Retraining will give you full control of your awareness, and a clear connection to it.

Simplicity

Hard as meditation may seem, the idea behind it – retraining your attention – is quite simple. This point is important because meditation is frequently shrouded in a cloud of mysticism and complex spiritual ideas. You may have heard about "seeing the white light" and "shifting into a different dimension". This is not what meditation is about. Although you may see a light or feel your consciousness shifting during meditation, these phenomena are not essential elements of the meditative experience. Meditation may lead to many joyful, painful, interesting, unique, or challenging moments, but then again it may not. Significantly, all these promises and expectations for unusual experiences only create another layer of ego concepts that interfere with actual meditation. It would be better if you regarded meditation as a *skill* that you are able to acquire, similar to riding a bike, or driving a car. These are both skills that give you the freedom of transportation; meditation is a skill that provides you with freedom of the mind. Remember, the meditative experience is basically very simple: bring your attention to the "here and now" (focus on anything), let go of any reactive thoughts, and stay there.

Patience and subtle changes

Meditation can really change the way you experience life, but a thorough change of this kind does not happen overnight. This point is highly important because inexperienced meditators imagine an immediate and complete transformation. Keep reminding yourself that investing time in meditation is similar to planting a raspberry bush; you plant it, watch it grow slowly, make fruit, and finally see the fruit ripen and enjoy its taste. At each stage you notice and enjoy some progress, and finally you savour the fruit. Patience is the name of the game; if you expect a complete transformation to occur after you have meditated for a week, you will be disappointed. Your mind patterns and the tendency to fluctuate have been there for years; you are now retraining your mind and should not expect your old habits to die in an instant.

Still, most of us notice *subtle* changes within a few weeks of daily practice. Once you start meditating, it is wonderful to observe how you begin noticing what you did not notice before: Your own emotions, reactions, and needs, as well as the attitudes of other people, and physical sensations such as the wind touching your skin or certain scents you never noticed before. First and foremost, you will start recognising the patterns of your own mind – the repetitive strings of ideas about certain issues in your life, and the behavioural and emotional responses that follow them. These all signal subtly that your attention has been expanding, and you may start noticing them just a few weeks after you begin meditating regularly. Psychological studies support this point. A team of researchers[14] found that 11 hours of meditation practice (spread over four weeks, up to 30 minutes per day) were sufficient to reveal differences in the participants' brain scans. The effects were seen in a region of the brain called the anterior cingulate cortex, an area that is in charge of self-control. It was found that the nerve fibres (also called white matter) became denser in that area, increasing the number of brain connections. Reduced activity in this region of the brain leads to mental problems such as depression, dementia, and attention deficit disorder. Therefore, increasing nerve activity by investing no more than 11 hours in meditation practice could help avoid mental problems of this kind. Another study[15] measured the cognitive influences of brief mindfulness meditation training. The participants were tested on a number of cognitive tasks, and were retested on the same tasks after undergoing four sessions of meditation training. It was found that these four sessions of meditation training reduced the levels of fatigue and anxiety, and improved memory and mindfulness. Studies of this kind show that subtle effects of meditation may be expected within the first few weeks of regular daily meditation practice. These changes brought about by meditation gradually invite you to change and grow. Self-awareness evolves and a clearer sense of direction, meaning, and transformation are experienced.

Psychological measurement 2: Personal growth initiative scale

The Personal Growth Initiative Scale[16] was developed to assess the level of personal growth in your life. It measures your own part in changing and developing as a person.

Instructions: Using the scale below, circle the number which best describes the extent to which you agree or disagree with each statement.

1	Definitely disagree
2	Mostly disagree
3	Somewhat disagree
4	Somewhat agree
5	Mostly agree
6	Definitely agree

1	I know how to change specific things that I want to change in my life.	
2	I have a good sense of where I am headed in my life.	
3	If I want to change something in my life, I initiate the transition process.	
4	I can choose the role that I want to have in a group.	
5	I know what I need to do to get started toward reaching my goals.	
6	I have a specific action plan to help me reach my goals.	
7	I take charge of my life.	
8	I know what my unique contribution to the world might be.	
9	I have a plan for making my life more balanced.	

Scoring: Personal Growth Initiative can be determined by summing the scores on all 9 items. Scores can range from 9 to 54, with higher scores indicating greater levels of intentional self-change.

Beginning to meditate
For most of us, the beginning of the meditative journey may be

accompanied by discomfort and struggle. The mind keeps bombarding you with information, ideas, protests, and temptations, and you are expected to simply sit, observe, and not react. Starting to meditate is sometimes challenging. We are used to search for distractions that mask the chaos and discomfort within; facebook, films, emails, anything to evade our internal commotion. And suddenly we meditate, and a huge mirror is put in front of us, reflecting our chaotic mind and the accompanying, restless, uncomfortable, feelings. Not only do we engage with these feelings as part of meditation, there is no escaping them; we are "stuck" with them for a while. This is the greatest difficulty in starting to meditate. But do not forget that these feelings and chaos you now begin to notice have been there anyway. Meditation has only created the space for you to *observe* them. Note also that one meditation session may differ from the other; you may experience bliss, peacefulness, deep relaxation, or vitality during the session or in its wake.

Different meditation sessions

You may realize that the experience of meditation changes frequently. You will most probably discover that it is practically impossible to predict how your daily practice will evolve. The sessions may be at times peaceful, and when you open your eyes you will be feeling tranquil and energised. You may then think "this is it, I've got it, I know how to meditate", only to find out that the following session may involve great difficulty and discomfort. These differences are completely natural, and simply reflect the shifts in your mind. You should recognise that meditation reflects whatever is truly happening within you at that point in time. Like the ocean, on certain days your mind is calm and peaceful and on other days it is stormy and chaotic. Meditation allows you to embrace the calm and the stormy with the same complete acceptance. The change you are seeking occurs as you acquire the capability to observe without interfering, regardless of your mood. You no longer depend on the shifts of your mind to feel calm; your tranquillity is based upon the new skill that you have developed, the skill of meditation.

Lesson 3: Aware and Unaware Thinking

The thinking obsession

Many of us are obsessed with certain things such as food, sex, gambling or work, or with certain people or emotions. When it comes to these obsessions we are out of control. But all of us have one obsession that we tend to ignore: we are obsessed with thinking. It is an obsession that escapes us because, even if we do not deny it, we take it for granted. Just as people might be obsessed with food and find themselves in front of the fridge without knowing how they got there; so it is with our mind and thinking. Thinking is our default state of consciousness. Unless a particularly powerful experience pulls our attention away and renders our mind "speechless", each and every activity we are involved in will always be accompanied by a stream of thought. This way of being seems natural, and is hardly ever an issue. But is there a different way of being? Obsession means being out of control. In the mind wandering exercise of lesson 2, I asked you to keep your attention focused on an object in a non-analytical way, to concentrate on it and keep it fully in your awareness without reacting to it in any way. How much time had passed before your attention was sidetracked by thinking? For most of us the answer would be no more than a few seconds. This is the span of your control over your thinking process. Thinking occurs automatically, and even when you consciously choose not to think, your attention becomes attached to a thought. Your conscious choice is overruled by thinking, which takes over your mind. Choosing a different object to focus on would make no difference; you might even scream in frustration: "Enough! I want to stop thinking right now, it is driving me crazy!" but you are unable to control your thoughts. Not only is this lack of control detrimental to your well-being, it also impairs your ability to be present.

There is nothing wrong with the mind

Our mind, that amazingly powerful and efficient instrument, was formed as part of our evolution. But it has since overpowered its owner. Instead of functioning as an instrument it is now the absolute ruler of our consciousness, the power that steers us and dominates our decisions and choices at each and every moment. In other words, we do not control our mind, and can no longer choose whether or not to use it at a particular moment.

Of course, we would have never been able to go through life without the help of the mind. When you make a grocery list you must know what your kids like to eat; when you drive over to the house of a friend, you must plan your route and mind the other drivers. Most of our daily activities involve using our mind. But what about all the other moments, when a call from within urges you to sit still, breathe, be meditative? The moments when you truly wish to listen to a friend peacefully, with deep presence? You soon find out that this is not possible. Your mind is so accustomed to react and think that you no longer have a choice. The mind throws in its automatic reaction at every moment, and your awareness is caught in it, whether you wish it or not.

Resting in your inner "home"

Imagine that meditation creates an inner space in you, which is calm and peaceful; this can be your inner "home". A space where you can stay, rest, let go of the burden of worries and calculations, and truly relax. This inner space is formed through regular practice of meditation, and is one of the best gifts you can offer yourself. By creating this space, you are actually offering yourself a choice: do I wish to engage in thinking or do I choose to stay in the peaceful space of my inner home? Here is a wonderful meeting point between psychology and spirituality. Psychology is essentially concerned with the cognitive processes of thinking, comparing, deciding; these processes denote very important moments in your life. Without them, life would be impossible. Spirituality, on the other hand, is essentially the experience of transcendence, that inner home, the space that takes us away from the processing of the mind and into a meditative space of peace; you breathe, your awareness turns inside, and you experience peace. In order to live your life fully, the most important skill you could strive for is the ability to move from one state to the other. The ability to engage with life in a cognitive way whenever this is required is essential. But the ability to engage with life meditatively is no less essential. A life devoid of thinking is complete chaos; but without meditation life would be marred by stress and anxiety. Having the option to choose between these two states results in an exquisite balance where psychology and spirituality both offer you the beauty of their presence in your life.

Aware vs. unaware thinking

Obviously, we are not talking about giving up thinking. But you do have a choice about the focus of your awareness. The point is regaining control over your awareness in order to be able to *choose*. Ask yourself: "Do I wish to think about what is happening right now, or do I simply want to be present while this moment unfolds? What would be the right choice for me?" At this stage, most of us never ask this question; we lack the skill to actually be present even if we wanted to. Once you cultivate your meditation skills your awareness will simply be present at the right moment. In other words, I invite you to switch from your currently unaware thinking, where your attention is automatically pulled away by your thoughts, to aware thinking, where you have the choice to consciously allow your attention to focus on your thoughts. Consider the following scenario: When I receive an email inviting me to give a talk on a certain date – I call forth my thinking faculty. I need to open my diary, check the dates, and make a choice. But what do I do next? If this were part of an aware thinking process, my awareness, having completed its analytical task, would again turn inward, waiting to be called again. Your awareness could focus on your breath, on your heart, or on any other meditative focal point. A minute or an hour later, you may choose to summon again your aware thinking to tackle another issue, and then let it go again. In other words, you choose the most suitable experience, whether meditation or thought, according to the requirement of the moment. But the traditional scenario is quite different. I use my mind to make a choice regarding the talk, but it does not end there. My mind immediately begins an endless parade of thoughts, some irrelevant, about the audience, the weather in the place where I give the talk, and the material I would like to expound on. This is a typical unaware thinking process. A relevant thought has triggered a series of mind reactions that sent my awareness spinning with thoughts that have nothing to do with the moment, and would only become relevant when I consciously choose to prepare for the talk. The thoughts that pulled me away from presence were ego-concept-based. The only moment that mattered was the one in which the decision about the talk was made. Would my awareness be strong enough to recognise that the thought process was completed and had to stop? Would I be able to let go of my thoughts and regain a state of peace? Or would I get entangled in a web of thinking?

Your self-growth will be expressed by your ability to transit smoothly from aware thought to meditative presence and back again, in an ongoing cycle, according to need. Awareness offers you the choice to switch from one to the other. Your own important task is to gradually evolve from unaware thinking into the process of aware thinking and cultivate your choice and freedom by doing that.

Cultivating aware thinking

How can you free yourself from being lost in your thoughts? To understand the answer we must examine the chain reaction of thought. Every thought that passes through your mind sets the background for the next one. Your attention keeps reacting to each thought in a way that makes way for the next. For example, you check your bank account and find out that your balance is £200. You immediately react with the thought: "That's much less than I expected", which, in it turn, invites: "I am so bad at managing my money"; this will trigger: "I should have taken that job"; and so on and so forth. You will come round five or fifty minutes later, realising that you were gone, submerged in this thinking process. This experience is entirely based on reaction. When I mentioned in lesson 2 that meditation means retraining your attention, I was referring to this reactive attitude, the automatic reaction to every moment, including events that are unfolding before your eyes, and thoughts that spring to your mind. To establish new relations with your thinking experience and develop aware thinking you must be able to break the cycle and develop the skill of non-reaction, the ability to come in touch with an event, a thought, a feeling, and having the choice of not reacting to them.

Here and now exercise 3: Writing your thoughts

Have pen and paper ready in front of you. Take a deep breath and relax your body. When you feel ready, start observing your thoughts. For two minutes, write down any thought that pops up in your mind, no matter how silly or meaningless it seems. The point of the exercise is to make you aware of your thoughts and not to evaluate them. If a new thought follows an earlier one write the new one as well. A thought may be as simple as "why am I doing this?" followed by "this might be beneficial". The exercise is meant to give you a taste of the type of observation required to master the non-reactive skill. All you have to do is keep observing and writing.

Ego concepts grow and shrink

An ego concept feeds on your reaction to it. Every time you react to a potential ego concept such as "I never do anything right" the concept becomes stronger. When the thought that you should do better at your work pops up in your mind, it triggers next the thought that you are unsuccessful in your job, and then the thought that you should have chosen a different job. Not only does this produce a chain reaction that pulls you off track for long minutes; it also builds up this particular ego concept. You are feeding the ego concept "I am unable to do things right" when you keep piling examples that seem to prove it, and make you feel even worse. You are on a rollercoaster of thoughts and ideas that energise not only this particular ride but also similar rides that may potentially occur under similar circumstances in the future.

If reaction strengthens an ego concept, what would it take to weaken it? *What would make it disappear?* In lesson 1 you were offered valuable insights about your ego concepts. You were shown how they influence your life and how they dictate your feelings and reactions. Becoming aware of them is profoundly important: it enables you to detect them when they kick in at different moments. Now you are ready to take the next step, and begin working with your ego concepts and eventually dissolve them. If reacting to an ego concept with an avalanche of thought strengthens the concept, then non-reactive attention would have the opposite effect. Ego concepts and the thoughts that accompany them thrive on the reactive attention they receive. When this stops, and your attention becomes non-reactive, you strangle them, starve them, until they slowly shrink and disappear. The moment you begin observing your thoughts non-reactively, observing your ego concepts, these thoughts slowly shrink and disappear – they no longer have anything to hold on to as you no longer fuel them as you did in the past. An ego concept is like a camp fire. Every time you react to it in any way, you add another piece of wood to the fire. A powerful emotional reaction would be a large piece of wood while a minor cognitive reaction would be a splinter, but both will feed the fire. The larger the fire is, the stronger your temptation to add wood to it. Your most powerful ego concepts are so strong that you feel you are compelled to react, to add the wood. As you grow, you will realise that your own reactions were the fuel that strengthened the fire, and will switch to non-reaction through meditation. Although the fire continues to blaze, inviting your consciousness to provide the vital wood, you are able to stay peacefully in front of the fire, and not strengthen it. With time, this camp fire will become smaller and smaller until at some point it will disappear. That particular ego concept will no longer have an impact on you.

Your reactive attention has been feeding your main ego concepts for years; they will not disappear in a day. But consistent non-reactive attention will gradually weaken them until they lose their powerful hold on your consciousness. In order to soar, this process must have two wings; the first is your attention, the second – your non-reactive attitude. Flapping only one would be meaningless: focusing your attention while reacting would only strengthen the pattern, and being non-reactive without being focused on the pattern would not make it shrink. Flapping both wings together would allow you to soar, fly towards freedom.

Gradual progress

The capacity to remain calm and centred, that is, to experience non-reactive awareness, takes time to develop. It is like a muscle which has been neglected for years, but would grow over time and strengthen with practice. Do not despair if you notice that you are frequently reacting at the beginning of the process. This makes sense. You have been reacting automatically for many years, and cannot expect this pattern to break immediately. Every month of consistent work and presence will make it slightly easier for you not to react, and remain calm and peaceful.

Breaking the attachment

Another important outcome of non-reactive attention is that it breaks the attachment between your awareness, your ego concepts, and your self. As you consistently observe and notice your thoughts and recognise your ego concepts, you will realise on an experiential level that your awareness is distinct from those thoughts and ego concepts.

This is a point we could discuss on a philosophical and intellectual level until the end of time. Even if you are reading these words and thinking to your self (notice, you *think* to your self, this is all happening in your mind) that your awareness is actually attached at the moment to your ego concepts, even if you accept this as a fact, you will not be able to break the attachment immediately. You will become aware that breaking the attachment is important and meaningful, but the break itself will not occur unless you *experience* non-attachment. Once you consciously notice the attached-ego-concept in your mind, you will also notice that your awareness is able to observe it, and realise that they are not the same thing. You could choose to have a different relationship with your thoughts, a non-reactive one. The more you put this relationship into practice, the closer you get to breaking the attachment, allowing yourself moments that are non-attached, and coming closer to life as it is.

Non-reactive attention

It is important to fully appreciate the meaning of the term "non-reactive attention". It means that when you focus your attention and observe a thought that reflects an ego concept, all you do is observe it, hold it in your consciousness, without rejecting it, craving it, or wishing for it to disappear, as these belong in the reactive mind, and only serve to intensify the thought. When you fight with a thought, pushing it away, grabbing it, or wishing for it to disappear and never come back, you achieve just the opposite: you feed and energise it. The only way to weaken it is by adopting a non-reactive attitude. You could think of meditation as the experience of the "watcher on the hill"; your awareness sits on top of the hill, observing the thought, but doing absolutely nothing about it. At some point the thought is likely to disappear and be replaced by a new one. As you proceed to watch this thought closely, without reacting to it, you will realize that its intensity is reducing, and it is loosening its grip on your awareness. You broke the cycle, refused to participate in the game of the mind, and consequently acquired a certain degree of freedom.

This is exactly why meditation is also known as the art of observation. Now you understand that the observation involved is the non-reactive kind. This is a crucial step in your spiritual journey. While your awareness discerns the parade of reactive thoughts in your mind, you gradually detach your awareness from the ego concepts these thoughts represent. You become free.

Psychological measurement 3: Relational Acceptance Questionnaire

One of the areas where we carry many attachments is relationships. We might be filled with ideas about the "right" and "wrong" way for our partner to be. On the other hand, we could be free of such attachments, filled with acceptance. The Relational Acceptance Quetionnaire[17] has been developed to assess the level of acceptance in a relationship – as expressed by both sides. As greater acceptance signifies reduced attachment it is a valuable measurement of attachment in an important dimension of life.

Instructions: Listed below are a series of statements about your relationship. Please choose the number, on a scale from 1 (strongly agree) to 5 (strongly disagree), which best expresses your level of agreement with each statement:

1	Strongly agree
2	Moderately agree
3	Do not agree nor disagree
4	Moderately disagree
5	Strongly disagree

1	I feel like my partner accepts me as a person, "warts and all."	
2	It feels like there are a lot of things that my partner wants to change about me.	
3	I frequently find myself thinking about things my partner does that I wish he/she would do differently.	
4	My partner is completely accepting of who I am, faults and mistakes included.	
5	It feels like I disappoint my partner a lot.	
6	I have a hard time getting over the times when my partner's behaviour disappoints me.	

7	My partner accepts my faults and weaknesses.	
8	My partner doesn't call my attention to my weaknesses.	
9	If I could magically remove all of the painful experiences I've had in my relationship, I would.	
10	My partner doesn't appreciate the "real me."	
11	I struggle to get my frustrations and disappointments about my partner under control.	
12	My partner makes me feel that he/she doesn't approve of me.	
13	I am comfortable just being myself around my partner.	
14	I have come to terms with things that once bothered or upset me in our relationship.	
15	When I am bothered by something about my partner, I can't stop thinking about ways he/she could change.	
16	I wonder if my partner really likes me.	
17	When my partner disappoints me, I am able to let it go.	

18	I would be okay with it if my partner couldn't change the things about him/her that bother me.	
19	My partner likes me for me.	
20	I often think about the problems my partner brings to the relationship.	
21	My partner always wants to change me.	
22	I don't dwell on my partner's weaknesses.	
23	My partner makes it clear he/she does not approve of me.	
24	I compare my partner to other individuals in order to figure out what is acceptable.	
25	I'm happy with my partner the way he/she is.	
26	I am able to take the bad with the good in my relationship.	

Scoring: Acceptance related questions are: 1, 4, 7, 8, 13, 14, 17, 18, 19, 22, 25, 26. Attachment (lace of acceptance) related questions are: 2, 3, 5, 6, 9, 10, 11, 12, 15, 16, 20, 21, 23, 24. Scores are obtained by summing up the scores of all relevant questions.

Pain is inevitable but suffering is optional

In our life, we are bound to have certain uncomfortable, even difficult experiences. What really makes a difference is whether or not we adopt the non-reactive way of being. As long as we react, our reactions will turn the originally uncomfortable moment into deep hurt, as we ignore the powerful chain of reaction, and the way it aggravates the difficulty. Take, for example the following simple experience: as you walk, your little toe bumps into the leg of a table. This is painful. The pain is a natural and important physiological reaction. But the following reactions are neither natural nor important: "I'm so clumsy" and "I told them the table is standing in the way and should be moved". Emotionally, you may feel angry and frustrated. These cognitive and emotional reactions amplify the original pain and make this experience considerably more difficult than it originally was. To put it simply: *Pain is inevitable but suffering is optional.* As long as you react, you choose to transform the pain into suffering. Non-reactive attention teaches you how to prevent your mind from falling into the pit of suffering. To this end, you must develop your meditative faculty, so that when you happen to bump your toe against the table, you just bring your attention to the pain and acknowledge it, doing nothing else until it subsides and disappears; this way you would avoid the potential string of thoughts and emotions with which you might have reacted.

To be able to take this step forward, you require the ability to observe without reacting, that is, the skill of meditation. You now understand how fundamental meditation is to spirituality and freedom; it is a prerequisite because it includes the quality of attention that frees you from the ego concepts, releases you from the illusionary self, and connects you with your Authentic Self.

Weekly exercise 3: Observing your thoughts

In the coming week you will have the opportunity to experience non-reactive observation by applying your meditative skills. For seven days, you will perform daily a ten minute practice that will begin modifying the current relationship of your awareness with your thoughts. During the first five minutes of the exercise note down your thoughts. As you did in the here and now exercise, note down any thought that comes to your mind. After five minutes drop your pen, close your eyes, and continue the same exercise in your mind. Simply observe your thoughts for five minutes, and notice how each comes up and what follows it. Some people prefer keeping their eyes open during the second part of the exercise. I suggest you experiment with both options.

In both parts of the exercise do your best not to react to any of the thoughts. If you find that you have been caught up in a string of thoughts, simply notice the way one has led to the other, and immediately resume your observation smilingly. With careful attention try to determine what generates a new thought, what is its source, and what keeps it alive.

Regular practice will help you notice experientially three important points:

- The actual meeting point between one thought and the next. You will find out that the tail of the original thought turns into the head of the following one.
- Focused non-reactive attention slowly weakens the intensity of the thoughts. The power they hold over your awareness will be reduced as will their ability to make your awareness wander. That will result from being attentive without feeding the thoughts with new material, new energy. As part of that experience you may even focus your full awareness but find no thoughts. Allow your awareness to be with this completely attentive state and remain alert.
- You and your thoughts are not one and the same, and your awareness is independent. This will slowly break the attachment between your awareness and you self and allow you to get in touch with life first hand.

Lesson 4: The illusion of the self

"Why are you unhappy?
Because 99.9 percent
of everything you think,
and everything you do,
is for your self,
and there isn't one."
Wu Wei Wei[18]

The concept of self

We are all aware of this thing we call "self". We picture our self as a concrete, solid entity that has great importance in our life. Moreover, many of us cannot conceive of a life without a self. Without a self, how can we experience life? Psychologically, the concept of self represents our fundamental drive to define ourselves. We create our self by listing the attributes, characteristics, and ideas that define us. This is the reason why in this book, a distinction is made between the terms Ego Formed Self and Authentic Self. These two notions are essentially different. Clearly, we all have a self that is all ours. It belongs to us, but it is not who we truly are. In this lesson we discuss this difference between the two, the meaning of this difference, and its implications.

The concept of self, as we commonly see it, is comprised of a series of psychological concepts and ideas which consist themselves of an organised collection of beliefs and emotions. In the present context, these concepts and ideas are the building blocks of your Ego Formed Self: who you are, what you are good at, what you believe in, when you would feel shy, what makes you angry. In other words, your ego concepts are not just floating around in your mind. They are well organised in a cohesive structure called your self. We have seen how ego concepts influence your experiences; similarly, your relationship with life depends upon this cohesive structure of ego concepts that makes up your Ego Formed Self. We now realise that whenever your consciousness encounters life, an organised entity that you call your self immediately interferes. This self is in charge of the interpretation of life discussed in lesson 1. We see now that the influence ego concepts have on the moment, and the interpretation they give rise to are not random but well organised. They are designed to support, sustain, and protect your self. Because whatever happens to us is interpreted through the filter of our Ego Formed Self we are unable to experience life as it is.

Trapped in patterns

Why are we trapped in patterns that keep repeating themselves? Past experiences and conditioning have gradually created in your mind a list of rights and wrongs, a series of understandings, expectations, and attitudes that define your Ego Formed Self and shape its building blocks. When you face certain situations – at work, with your partner, or with your family – your Ego Formed Self kicks off preconceived reactions, organised responses that reflect a certain aspect of it. We are rarely able to choose our response; the response is already there before you come in touch with the moment, it is embodied in your Ego Formed Self. And that is why you are trapped in a pattern of recurring emotional reactions, always pushing away and attracting similar people and situations. There is no magic here, no underlying metaphysical law; it is simply the outcome of the rigidly constructed manner by which your Ego Formed Self approaches life, producing a similar result time and again. All these characteristics, expectations, and ideas have been welded together to create the greatest obstacle standing in your way to freedom – your own self.

Not only do your accumulated ego concepts perpetuate these patterns, they also restrict your own perspective of life and set limits to your self. By adopting certain ego concepts you define your self but at the same time you define what you are *not*. For example, if you carry a schema that defines you as insensitive, your self would reject the very notion of sensitivity. At the relevant moment the option of being sensitive will not be at your disposal. Numerous ways of being are simply not available to you because your self is not programmed to accommodate them. By limiting your self this way, you are limiting your capacity to face life as it is. So many situations are outside your comfort zone simply because you have defined your self in a certain way, and you now lack the tools that could potentially show you how to deal with the moment as it is. An example could be the issue of feminine and masculine qualities in a person – male or female. All males and females have both masculine and feminine qualities, but are mostly conditioned to adopt only those that match their gender. Most of us feel that we must make a choice. We can be either this or that. Once this choice is made, our experience of life necessarily becomes more restricted, as certain moments require an interaction that is feminine-like, and others, the opposite. Psychological research indicates that the ability to contain both the feminine and the masculine within you has many advantages. In one of my studies[19], participants who scored high in both the masculine and feminine scales also displayed higher levels of self-actualisation, that is, better fulfilment of their potential. These findings suggest that the capacity to embrace both aspects of your self rather than regard them as mutually exclusive directly impacts your capability to live your life in full. This can only be achieved if you let go of your ego concepts about masculinity or femininity. As long as you are not burdened with such preconceptions you have the capacity to apply each of those qualities to suit the moment.

Is there a "container"?

Being human means having sensations, expectations, ideas, beliefs, and experiences. Together, all these elements form your Ego Formed Self. It is tempting to imagine the self as a container, where these expectations and ideas are stored in a coherent manner. Spirituality, however, questions the existence of such a "container". It maintains that there is no "you", or self, that retains these sensations and ideas. What, then, are we? The answer is that *you are* those sensations, ideas, and experiences. Your awareness and the experience become one if no ego concepts stand in the way. And in the next moment, your awareness unites with another sensation, and becomes one with it, in an unending sequence. But the mind is extremely uncomfortable with this kind of idea because it robs it of its interpretive role. And so, it reacts and begins its story telling. It weaves a narrative, a plot, to make sense of different experiences and ideas, and bring them together to form a clear story. That story is your self.

To elucidate this point, let us compare the self to a house. We all agree that a house is made of parts such as walls, windows, doors, and a roof. No one would suggest that there is an additional separate entity called a house. All the components come together to make a house, and the house is not an independent entity that exists *in addition* to the components.

This is also an issue where spirituality and psychological and other scientific research complement and support each other. Buddhism embraces the concept of Annata, which in the Pali language means "no-self". This concept stands for the idea that our sense of a solid self, discussed above, is simply an illusion. Contemporary philosophy, psychology, and neuroscience indicate the same. The philosopher Thomas Metzinger[20], for example, said "modern philosophy of mind and cognitive neuroscience together are about to shatter the myth of the self". Neuropsychology, which links the functioning of the brain with psychological processes, mainly supports this point because the self is not found anywhere in the brain. The meaning of this must be fully understood. If we go back to the house metaphor, we could say that neuropsychology shows that specific brain areas are in charge of the "walls" and other specific areas deal with the "windows" or process the "roof", but there is no specific area where they all come together to create a "house". The house is a term we have coined to join together the walls, windows, and roof, in a way that would make sense to us. It is perfectly fine to talk about a house as an abstract concept that enables referring to this place where you live – as long as you accept that in reality, it is merely a combination of walls, windows and a roof. The same applies to neuropsychological research concerning the self. Areas in the brain have been identified for many of our experiences (sensations, cognitive processes, emotions, etc.) but no area has been identified as our self, where all of those experiences are joined together to form one entity. I find the house an appropriate metaphor for the self because both concepts represent a safe space comprised of components that are important to us. We struggle to make a distinction between the concrete components and the name we gave the container, which, in fact, is an illusion. The neuroscientist Paul Broks says: "we have this deep intuition that there is a core, an essence there, and it's hard to shake off – probably impossible to shake off, I suspect. But it's true that neuroscience shows that there is no centre in the brain where things do all come together." [21]

We have no difficulty acknowledging that the objects around us (such as the house) do not exist independently of their components. However, when it comes to us, our approach suddenly changes. When we refer to our own existence, we tend to believe that all these parts (experiences, sensations, beliefs), which actually exist, are all kept in a separate container we call our self. To us, this separate entity we call "the self", seems to exist independently of its parts, and significantly impacts our relationship with life, as it leads to separation.

Separation

An important outcome of the concept of Ego Formed Self is a built-in separation between your awareness and the experience of the moment. At any given moment, we are invited to have an experience and be with it. If we were to accept the invitation, we would experience the situation as it is, and be fully connected to it. Smelling a flower would mean being consumed by the scent. Nothing else would be there, no thoughts about the scent, no expectations and wishes but simply a total connection to the experience of smell, and to being one with the scent. In spirituality the idea of oneness is frequently said to be essential for understanding life. Spiritual oneness is the actual experience of a moment where the self does not interfere with or break the unity between the activity and our awareness of it. Awareness becomes one with the experience of the moment. It is a moment when you get a glimpse of life that is not distorted by your automatic cognitive reactions to it, where you transcend the meta-cognition, the reactive thoughts to your cognition, and have your attention fully submerged in the experience.

This is where the idea of duality is easily understood. As long as the mind takes control of the experience, your awareness and the moment can never bond and become one. The mind, in its role as a messenger of the Ego Formed Self, automatically produces duality, throwing another player into the moment – the Ego Formed Self, with its requirements, needs, expectations, and ideas. We then face duality, a clash between the moment and its interpretation by the Ego Formed Self. This is the cause of our difficulty, the reason why we keep saying "no" to life. Because our Ego Formed Self is burdened with so many ideas about the way things are *supposed* to be, more often than not the encounter between the moment and the Ego Formed Self means conflict. We keep rejecting what the moment has to offer by letting our ideas about how it should be interfere with it. This conflict creates inner discomfort. We feel that something is wrong with our life, that it is not going in the right direction and is too difficult. What really happens is that duality, this automatic creation of the mind, affects our experience of life in a way that leads to conflict. It is the primary conflict between what it is and what we think it should be.

A study I have run provides an example for the influence of our self concepts on our wellbeing, and the impact of mindfulness meditation on that process.[22] To make my point, I used the psychological Self Discrepancy Theory (SDT), which describes a number of self-conceptions; I focused on two of them:

1 Actual self – representing the attributes individuals actually identify in themselves.
2 Ideal self – representing the attributes individuals would ideally like to possess.

In spiritual terms, these are two examples of ego concepts. The first refers to the way you define yourself and the second – to what you aspire to be. SDT stands for the gap between these two dimensions of the self. What would the consequences be, if the ego concepts of which your actual self is made did not match the ones you see as your ideal self? Psychological research indicates that a gap of this kind results in dissatisfaction and depressive symptoms. This makes sense: If you imagine your self in a certain way but would like it to be different, this would naturally result in discontent. This is a classic example of an internal clash between ego concepts and its negative psychological consequences.

In my study, I examined the influence of mindfulness meditation on the gap between these two ego concepts. I assumed that an influence of this kind actually exists, because meditation has been shown to improve the levels of self-acceptance for reasons that are discussed later on. The important point is that meditation often creates a healthier relationship with one's concept of self, and increases one's self- acceptance. The idea naturally follows that it may also help resolve the SDT issue. The purpose of the research was to determine the impact a weekend of intensive mindfulness meditation retreat had on SDT in a group of 120 participants. Self-discrepancy levels were measured before and after the meditation retreat and the differences between them were evaluated. As expected, the results showed that the gap narrowed significantly following the mindfulness meditation retreat. Meditation appeared to prompt a psychological transformation that allowed the participants to feel more comfortable with themselves. How did this happen? Mindfulness meditation invites us to relate to our thoughts in a non-attached manner. Observe, notice, and avoid reacting to the thought. Self-discrepancy is a cognitive phenomenon: The idea of who I am clashes with the idea of who I would like to be, resulting in psychological discomfort. This discomfort occurs when your mind is preoccupied with thoughts about the gap. Mindfulness meditation breaks this thought pattern. Relating to our thoughts in a non-attached way breaks this vicious circle; engagement with thoughts regarding the actual and ideal self is significantly reduced and the gap experience weakens. This study illustrates the way meditation diminishes our engagement with our ego concepts, allowing a healthier attitude towards the self. In other words, it allows diminishing the engagement with the self concepts that intervene with the moment and pull your awareness from oneness with it.

Most of us rarely experience oneness with the moment. The Ego Formed Self immediately interferes and separates our awareness from the experience, breaking their momentary bond. Contemplate, for example, a moment where you watch the blue sky. At that moment your mind separates the object being watched (the blue sky) from the observer (your self); but this separation results from your thinking reaction to the moment. If you relate to the moment as it is, there is nothing left but a blue sky; your awareness is submerged in it, and as long as you transcend analysis by the mind, you become one with the blue sky. The same applies, for example, to hearing. You may have been to a classical music concert where the music, the sound, engulfed you, and you felt you were "lost" in it. What you lost was the idea of self. For a moment you were able to let go of the ever-present commentating Ego Formed Self and let your awareness unite with the moment, the music.

Here and now exercise 4: Can you find the experiencer?

We begin the exercise with an auditory experiment. Experiential testing is the best tool of education. The Buddha used to say that we are walking experiment labs, in which we are both running the experiment and participating in it. So, let's run the experiment. Relax your body, close your eyes, breathe deeply, and focus your attention on your hearing. Spend a minute focusing on whatever you are hearing. Notice the different sounds you detect. Once you are comfortable with the sounds, search inside you for the experiencer, a discrete part of you that is actually engaged in hearing. Can you find it?

You may try the same exercise with your vision. Focus your attention on a certain object and notice as many details as you can about it. When you are comfortable with the object, search inside you for the part that is the experiencer, the seer. Can you find it? Are you able to detect a discrete part that sees the object and yet is detached from it?

I recommend that you do not answer the question intellectually. Try to find the answer in your own experience and not analytically. An analytic approach will immediately bring in ego concepts that will interfere with your insight and pronounce it possible or impossible. The experience itself has much more to teach you than thinking about it.

This little experiment might be perplexing. Is it at all possible to search and find this thinker? Is it possible for you to locate the thinker that thinks "I'm perplexed" or can you only find the thought "I'm perplexed"? You will realize that by trying to search for the experiencer you will only stir up other thoughts. We are unable to separate the thinker from the never-ending flow of thought. The thought and the thinker are identical. When you look at the sky there is no distinction between the experience of "sky" and the experience of "seeing the sky". They are an inseparable single experience that is being divided in your mind as a result of your self concept. The self, therefore, does not exist outside the experience.

Note that, in fact, sensations, feelings, and thoughts all exist, but we have welded them together and pretend they make up an entity that does not really exist – the self. Our experiences are not an illusion; but the story we have created to bind them together is. Perhaps it would be easier to visualize this as a story. We go through life holding on to a solid belief that there is a self made of various components. Just as every good story, this one also has a beginning followed by numerous experiences that reach to the current moment. The spiritual idea of no-self maintains that every moment in your story is true, but wrapping them all together into one packet you call your self, is an illusion. And this illusion is a major obstacle in your path towards freedom, constantly interfering with the moment as it is.

"The sense of self, such that you know yourself as distinct from the armchair, is a functional reality. What happens in humans is that at the age of roughly 2 1/2, this sense of self gets hijacked by a false sense of self-as-the-author (FSA). The FSA is like ivy that grows up a tree and finally covers it to the point that you can't imagine the tree without the ivy. To get rid of the ivy you conclude you must chop down the tree. But if you chop down the tree what is left to experience? However, if you get rid of the ivy you are left with a beautiful, healthy tree to enjoy. The sense of self without its covering of parasitic FSA is truly a thing of beauty."

Wayne Liquorman[23]

Attachment to the self

You may have come across the concept of "non-attachment" as

part of the spiritual teaching canon. We become attached to our Ego Formed Self via the ego concepts that make it. You are so strongly attached to your ego concepts that you link every moment of your life, your whole existence, with them. The occasions on which your awareness is free of them are rare, and you therefore go through life without being directly connected with it. You get used to seeing those ego concepts as your self because you are so attached to them. By "developing a non-attached relationship with life" I mean being able to let go of the powerful link between your awareness and your ego concepts. Just as the participants in the meditation retreat did when they experienced a reduced self-discrepancy gap. When you do that you stop seeing those ego concepts as your self and gain a certain degree of freedom.

I am not discussing this idea at such length merely because of its philosophical interest. What is wonderful about ideas is that they often transform into insights that can be applied in everyday life. If they merely remain ideas they are nothing but words. A major change can only occur where a new idea meets actual life. As long as an idea does not touch upon your actual experiences, the chance for change and transformation is drastically reduced. Therefore, the discussion of Ego Formed Self is not philosophical; it has important implications for the way we live our life. Understanding this point is extremely important, considering that we invest endless efforts in strengthening and supporting something that *does not really exist*. You try so hard to take on many ego concepts, and thus make sure that *you* are "this" but not "that", while this *you* does not exist. Not only do you invest much time and energy in creating the Ego Formed Self, you then miss its impact, the way it interprets the moment and clashes with it.

In practice, once you recognise that the Ego Formed Self is an illusion, this recognition will have an impact on the central place this self has in your life. If your Ego Formed Self was once a huge issue that had to be considered constantly, it now occupies its rightful place – merely another process of the mind, similar to many other thoughts and ideas. The feeling that this "me" is dominant and ever-present slowly dissipates, and the Ego Formed Self becomes understated, having lost the power it used to have over your consciousness. When this happens, the ego concepts of which the self is made naturally lose some of the urgency and importance they used to carry, making space in your awareness for direct interaction with the experience.

The mind fights for its existence

It is very difficult to grasp these ideas about the self because the entire discussion stems from the mind, where the concept of self is formed, and also goes on in it. The sequence of reasoning is the following:

- Ego concepts create an Ego Formed Self in your mind, that you experience as a self.
- You conclude that you will cease existing if you let go of your ego concepts because ego concepts, the self, and your existence are one and the same.
- You think this way because this whole reasoning goes on in your own mind. For the mind, to let go of its ego concepts means to let go of its very building blocks.
- Therefore, the mind fights for its existence.

This point explains the great difficulty encountered in spiritual discussions: We try to understand the illusion of the mind by using the mind! We try to discuss issues related to the inadequacies of a certain tool while using the tool itself to understand them. This is the paradox of spiritual teaching, and that is why it is more important and beneficial to *experience* spiritual teaching than *think about* it. By thinking about this teaching you are trapped in the paradox of using the mind to contemplate the illusion it creates. To become directly connected to the spiritual themes you must experience them. A moment of oneness with your breath will bring you much closer to freedom than a full-day workshop where you *think* about oneness. This emphasises the importance of meditation, of spiritual transcendence. The meditative experience teaches us how to engage with life while moving beyond the interpretive mind, and how to bypass thinking when necessary.

Enlightenment: an alternative to the Ego Formed Self

The concept of spiritual enlightenment is among the spiritual concepts that are most frequently contemplated, and often awakens controversy. An enlightened way of being represents the essence of spiritual transcendence. It means living a life in which analysis by the mind is continuously transcended, evading any interference. An enlightened existence means oneness with experiences, devoid of any duality, where the self is known to be an illusion, and life is experienced completely independently of it. This state has been given different names. It is referred to, for example, as the state of Nirvana, Unity Consciousness, Samadhi, Awakening, and Enlightenment. Whatever name is used, what matters is that it is regarded as a state of freedom from the tyranny of the mind and the illusion of the self. Do you remember yourself as a child? You were basically fearless, intrinsically willing to say "yes" to the adventure of life. At that time you had an incredible ability to let go of any difficulty, you were able to move smoothly from one experience to another because you never identified your self with any of them. We often see two children fight as if they were the worst enemies on earth, and a minute later they play together as if they were the greatest friends. This demonstrates the ability of children to switch effort-lessly from one moment to the next without emotional response. Each moment is tackled separately and completely as a whole. This is a wonderful manifestation of the state of enlightenment. This state is frequently referred to as the Authentic Self. It is authentic because it is the original state of the self, in which it was an empty vessel that allowed living life as it is rather than trying to shape it according to the self's concepts of right and wrong. We are all born enlightened; as years go by we keep accumulating self concepts, and slowly move away from that primary innocence, from the deep feeling that life could be anything and everything. With every bit of conditioning our experience of life, which originally embraced whatever came its way, slowly shrinks to accommodate the limitations of our own mind and self. For some of us this may begin earlier than for others, and the rate of accumulation and conditioning is individual. But this learning process is inescapable, and we unavoidably move away from our original state of enlightenment and enter a state of illusion.

I say that this process is inescapable as it is truly impossible to avoid this conditioning at a very young age. In many ways, the entire spiritual journey is based upon that learning and conditioning – because at a certain point along the way, you begin the process of unlearning. This may happen at different points in life, at different ages, and for a variety of reasons, but the connecting thread is the deep feeling that "I am not experiencing life's gifts in full". This is a nagging feeling that tells you that you have lost what you once had as a young child. That you are reading this book is a sign that you have awakened to the fact that your life has been incomplete. Something within you, the core of your Authentic Self, is inviting you to recall your awareness and return home, to let go of illusion and pretence, and regain your original state. This is when the journey of unlearning begins; the journey whereby you strip yourself of the layers in which you have been wrapped, like an onion, to reveal, at the end, your Authentic Self.

This idea is tremendously challenging. You might be thinking: "Nothing? I am nothing? How could that be?" And yet remember that this nothingness was the foundation of freedom during childhood. Back then, free of definitions and expectations, you experienced life as an adventure. The present book invites you to walk the path of unlearning by recognizing all you have learned (psychology) and then transcending it (spirituality). In lesson 3 we discussed and practiced the way becoming aware of your mind patterns allows you to let go of your grip on them, unlearn them, and allow them to shrink and disappear. By reading on and regularly engaging in the exercises, you will have begun your process of unlearning, whether you recognise it or not.

Awareness of the layers that conceal your Authentic Self

To connect with your Authentic Self and experience enlightenment, you need not learn anything. This is your natural way of being; it is who you are underneath the layers of different ego concepts you have accumulated. But you will have much to unlearn, because anything new you learn will simply turn into new layers you will later have to discard. The sooner you find the way to let go of these layers, the smoother will your journey be from your Ego Formed Self to your Authentic Self. As you shed the unnecessary wrappings of the Ego Formed Self you will naturally come closer to your Authentic Self, your authentic way of being, where you experience true freedom. You may find it now easier to appreciate the importance of psychology in this process. These layers exist all on a psychological level. The concepts that you have accumulated are very personal and may make you feel vulnerable: "I am worthless", "Life only works for me when I am very cautious; people will hurt me if I'm not", "Everything good ends in pain". Those are all ego concepts, layers, that you will let go of as part of your unlearning process. But it is very hard to let go of that which you don't know. Awareness, therefore, is the key to your awakening and freedom. It allows you to identify your most powerful layers and start working towards shedding them. Once you become aware of these layers you will realize how attached you are to them, how enslaved you are to your predictable and automatic responses. That is the reason why awareness is at the basis of the growth process; that is why *awareness is freedom.*

Facing your self

Becoming aware of the layers that wrap your Authentic Self is an important stage – and an uncomfortable one. In the process, you have to face all the dimensions of your Ego Formed Self that you may prefer to hide, repress, and look away from. That is why growing takes much courage, the courage to face your Ego Formed Self. You must acknowledge the components your Ego Formed Self is made of, the things you have learned and accumulated along the years. Some of the concepts you have adopted might be painful to engage with, because they were formed in painful moments of your life. For example, one might carry an underlying ego concept that says "People hurt me; I should not open up to them". This ego concept may have sprung from a trauma of abandonment by a partner, or the death of a close family member. It might have been an important psychological defence mechanism that served the individual at that point in time. However, we frequently continue to carry this defence mechanism and continue applying it to future events where it is no longer relevant or needed. With time, it has become a powerful ego concept making this person navigate his or her relationship with life through the filter of this view. This view is frequently not conscious and its impact is unknown to that person. And here comes your challenge: know thy self. Explore those aspects of your self and try to *recognise* and *accept* the existence of those layers. Remember, *only that which has been recognised can be transcended.* How are you expected to transcend something that you are not aware of? How can you let go of something that is working, unconsciously, from within your mind? Here, again, is a meaningful meeting point between psychology and spirituality. The first enables recognising the building blocks of your Ego Formed Self; the second invites you to transcend them. Together, they offer freedom.

What is the experience of enlightenment?

At certain moments you experience transcendence, and catch a glimpse of life as it is. These moments occur when, for some reason, there is a break in the ongoing activity of your mind. When this activity stops, for a brief moment you experience something completely different. This could occur under various circumstances: Deep meditation, extreme shock, an orgasm, the influence of a drug, or an amazingly beautiful natural phenomenon. All these moments have one thing in common: They bring your mind's activity to a halt, they press the "pause" button for a while. What do you feel when this happens? Imagine that underneath the never-ending commentary of the mind, underneath all the layers of the Ego Formed Self, runs an under-current. This undercurrent is filled with feelings of unconditional love, peace, compassion, and joy. And this undercurrent is constantly calling you, with every breath you take. It is vibrating inside you, because it is who you really are. It is an inner call to return home, to the point where you started and where you will end. Your Ego Formed Self and its ego concepts form a thick layer that makes it very difficult for you to experience that under-current under regular circumstances. To break through the thick layer of the mind and dip in these waters, you actually need those rare moments. Have you ever found yourself filled with love or joy or peace that was so immense you almost could not contain it? That was a moment of connection to the source, to the under-current, to your Authentic Self; a moment of enlightenment. And the beauty of it is that it may happen suddenly and unexpectedly. You could be standing on the top of a mountain, watching the horizon, or standing on the beach watching the waves, and suddenly something clicks; you stop thinking and come in touch with your Authentic Self. You become one with this amazing, deep, acceptance and joy, knowing deep within that everything is perfectly fine, has always been, and will always be. A few heartbeats later, the mental noise that gave in for a moment regains control over your awareness and tears your awareness away from the connection to the undercurrent.

Psychological measurement 4: Compassion Scale

A frequently discussed attribute of the Authentic Self is a deep feeling of compassion. Caring and relating to others, even when they are strangers, is at the heart of enlightenment. It is easy to contemplate the reason for that: when the barriers between the personal self and all others fall away, the individual recognises itself as being part of the whole. When that happens, connecting, empathising, relating, and caring, flow naturally. The Santa Clara Brief Compassion Scale[24] measures the level to which compassion is felt.

Instructions: Please answer the following questions honestly. Choose an answer ranging from 1 (not at all true of me) to 7 (very true of me).

1	Not at all true of me
2	
3	Slightly true of me
4	
5	Moderately true of me
6	
7	Very true of me

1	When I hear about someone (a stranger) going through a difficult time, I feel a great deal of compassion for him or her.	
2	I tend to feel compassion for people, even though I do not know them.	
3	One of the activities that provide me with the most meaning to my life is helping others in the world when they need help.	
4	I would rather engage in actions that help others, even though they are strangers, than engage in actions that would help me.	
5	I often have tender feelings toward people (strangers) when they seem to be in need.	

Scoring: To score the scale, calculate the arithmetic mean of the five items. Higher scores stand for a higher level of compassion.

Weekly Exercise 4: Consciously choosing enlightenment

What would happen if you could practice meditation and invite more of these glimpses of enlightenment? In this week's exercise you will make a conscious attempt to press the "pause" button, shift from the ongoing activity of the mind, and experience a glimpse of enlightenment, a moment of deep, present awareness. If you go over the list of moments in which people tend to experience enlightenment you will discover that most of them are far from ordinary. Would it be possible to create a shift in our awareness that involves the mundane, everyday life experiences? In order to increase the occurrence of glimpses of this kind in your everyday life, I ask you to exercise my "Shifting Attention" Meditation, every day for a week.

- Sit comfortably.
- Take three deep breaths, and relax your body as you exhale. You are simply preparing your mind and body for the meditation.
- Close your eyes and practice for one minute your breathing meditation. If you have another favourite meditation technique, feel free to use it. To measure time you can either set up an alarm clock for one minute or count 15 breaths. You can also roughly estimate the time – it makes no difference if this part is slightly longer or shorter than one minute.
- When the minute is up, open your eyes and focus your attention on task assessment; start thinking about the different tasks you must complete today and tomorrow: where do you have to go, who you must call, where you must drive the kids, what bills you have to pay, which responsibilities you have to deal with at work, and what food you should buy at the grocery store. Dedicate one minute to this part as well.
- Close your eyes and move into meditation for one minute, and then go back to your task assessment for another minute.
- The session is concluded when you complete three rounds of meditation and task assessment.
- In addition to this daily practice session, apply the meditation as frequently as you can to the experiences of your day by consciously choosing to shift your attention from the mind's assessments to meditation and back. You can do this while you are arguing with a friend, as you walk outside, and while you stand in a queue; whenever you notice you are involved in task assessment,

consciously shift to a moment of meditation before you move back to the assessment.

- Practice this exercise regularly and you will gain the freedom to choose, and shift between, doing (activity of striving or thinking) and being (surrender, peace, meditation).

Taking a step back from the never-ending chatter of the mind is one of the greatest difficulties we face in our life. This exercise will teach you how to consciously break the entanglement with your daily task assessment. By creating such gaps in your insistent thinking patterns you will consciously invite glimpses of enlightenment. The important insight I would like to share with you is that enlightenment may occur in places other than the top of a mountain after 20 years of non-stop meditation. You could get a glimpse of enlightenment right after that meeting with your boss, when your mind is filled with reactions and bouncing thoughts, and you consciously choose to close your eyes, shift your attention inwardly to meditate, and find deep tranquillity within. This is enlightenment and it awaits you at any moment of your everyday life.

Lesson 5: Everything is Neutral

We have discussed the ego concepts we carry in our minds, the way by which they create the Ego Formed Self, and their influence on our relationship with life. A number of psychological theories will help us understand the way our assumptions and past experiences interfere with our perception of the moment and determine the way we store it in our memory.

Here and now exercise 5: The clock experiment

Let us make a little experiment. You will need pen and paper, and may wish to invite the people around you to participate as well. When you are through reading this paragraph, take a close look at the picture of the clock. Watch it for 60 seconds and then turn the page over and follow the instructions.

Now, take a few minutes to draw the clock you have just watched. Include in your drawing every detail you remember.

When you are through, go back to the original picture. Are there any significant differences between your drawing and the original picture? This little experiment was part of a study[25] that was based on the fact that in clocks with roman numerals, the digit 4 is replaced by IIII and not by IV, its conventional representation. Although we have all seen many clock faces with 4 represented as IIII, most of us would represent 4 by IV immediately after having watched closely the face of the clock. In this study, 66% of the participants who were asked to memorise the clock made that mistake.

Schema theory

The results of this experiment are explained by the psychological schema theory, which maintains that previous knowledge has an important role in shaping the data our memory is taking in. All our knowledge, such as knowledge related to people, events, objects, situations, etc., is organised in our brain in packets of information or schemas. Schema theory contends that the schemas existing in the mind enter into action when we try to recall information, and take over our memory processes. In the clock experiment, for example, our inability to recall the IIII correctly is explained by the schema theory. In reconstructing the information, we do not refer exclusively to the mental image of the clock. Instead, we are likely to fill the gaps with any available schematic knowledge. In this case, the digit 4 is represented by IV in our schematic knowledge. This schematic knowledge is so powerful that it overrides the actual image of the clock. What we actually do is use our past experience and knowledge to restructure our memories. In psychology, this is defined as "reconstructive memory": An active mental process where the information being recalled combines with previous knowledge and experiences. This is an inadvertent process that results in a distorted memory of whatever has happened. A classic psychology experiment carried out by Bartlett[26] as part of his study of reconstructive memory provided a good example of this phenomenon. Bartlett presented the participants of his experiment, all white Americans, with a series of drawings, paintings, and poems. After several days, weeks, months, and even years, he asked them to reproduce the materials they had been shown. A story called "The war of the ghosts", based upon the Native American culture, illustrated perfectly the point he was trying to make. Because this story originated in a culture that was thoroughly different from that of the participants, it clashed with their own schemas. Bartlett found significant distortions in the participants' reconstruction of the story, which kept growing with time. Most importantly, the distortions tended to be influenced by the participants' own culture. The participants' schemas were gradually taking over, and their recollection of the story increasingly leaned on their own cultural background, discarding the original Native American features.

Priming

The influence of ego concepts does not end with reshaping our memories. Ego concepts also shape our relationship with every moment of our life. The psychological concept of *priming* best illustrates this process. You are said to be primed when a past stimulus affects your response to a later stimulus. Psychological studies show that subtle hints coming from certain words and concepts are capable of bending your behaviour in their direction. In 1996, John Bargh and his colleagues[27] asked the participants of a study they were conducting to form sentences from a store of scrambled words. The participants were divided into two groups. The first group was given words that included the words "old", "bingo", "wrinkle", "gray" and "lonely", all words that we associate with old age. The second group received no words from this semantic field. The participants were then sent down the hall to complete another task, but they did not know that their walk down the hall was being timed. The results were amazing: The first group took significantly longer to walk down the hall than the second group. This led to the conclusion that the participants of the first group were primed by the words associated with old age, and their ego concepts about getting old were triggered. Their predictions, beliefs and ideas regarding the experience of getting old came alive in their mind, and had a direct impact on their behaviour, making them walk more slowly. This example is a good illustration of the connection between your ego concepts and your bearing. The ego concepts embedded in your mind are triggered by words, ideas, images, and people you happen upon in different situations, and interfere with your conscious and unconscious behaviour. Most significantly, this process is not conscious, and you are unaware of it. If you asked the participants of the first group why they were walking more slowly they would not know what you were talking about. Similarly, a situation you believe to be reality as it is actually a product of your ego concepts shaped by your beliefs and expectations. Let me give you another example: Imagine that you are opening a new dental practice. Are you going to refer to your patrons as "customers" or "patients"? This distinction is crucial, as every person working in the practice (including you) will approach the patrons differently, according to the way they are regarded; "customers" will be primarily viewed from a business perspective while "patients" will be viewed from a care-giving perspective. This indicates that the labels "customers" and "patients" trigger each a different ego concept or schema in your mind. Each incorporates different attitudes, expectations, and beliefs, generating a different behaviour. As already mentioned, most of this process happens unconsciously, and you will not be aware of the way the priming (the choice of name for the patrons) triggers an ego concept that determines the way you approach the patron. Processes of this kind occur every moment of your life; you are continuously primed by your accumulated ego concepts, and react automatically. The question is how aware you are of the roots of your choices, and how many of your reactions are based upon triggered ego concepts that influence your approach to a certain situation. In the course of your psychological journey you will see these unconscious processes gradually become conscious. Unless you are fully aware of your motivations you will find it hard to see yourself as autonomous and free.

As a result of this recurring process, we keep shaping our reality in a way that "proves" our beliefs, thoughts and assumptions to be ostensibly right. A psychological theory that illustrates this point is that of the self-fulfilling prophecy. This theory suggests that schemas are reinforced by situations involving the person/place/thing they relate to. For example, if one of my schemas maintains that North-European women are not smart, this will influence the way I behave in the company of a Scandinavian girl: I will probably not ask her interesting questions or listen to her with attention. As a result, the girl would feel uncomfortable and close up, giving the impression that she is indeed uninteresting. The prophecy has fulfilled itself. Our approach to a specific moment is influenced by the schema (ego concept) and shapes it accordingly. In turn, this strengthens the original schema, and here we are, entrapped in an ever growing false understanding of the world, that hinders us from seeing life as it is.

Spirituality and schemas

A fundamental spiritual insight maintains that life is a mirror that reflects your mind. In a famous Buddhist story, two monks had an argument about the temple's flag that was blowing in the wind. The first monk contended that the flag was moving, while the other insisted that the wind was the one to move. They went on arguing heatedly until a third monk overheard them and said that neither the flag nor the wind was moving, but the mind. Not only does the mind interpret every moment, in doing so it follows your most powerful ego concepts. When this happens, you perceive the moment as it was shaped by your ego concepts. This explains the mirror-like nature of your life: if you shape each moment according to your own assumptions, beliefs, and understandings, you should be able to identify them by closely examining the moment. Here is an example from my own experience. In a yoga class I have attended, several students used to wear spotted swimming suits. The teacher, who did not know their names, addressed them by this feature: "The girl with the spots in the back row, lock your elbows". The student replied defensively: "It's because of the mosquitoes". The teacher was obviously referring to the girl's spotted swimsuit, while the girl thought he was referring to the spots on her skin. The girl interpreted reality according to her most powerful ego concepts ("everyone thinks my skin looks horrible, people often make fun of me or of the way I look"). Had she been an aware individual she would have recognised the reflection of these ego concepts in the situation; she would have been able to observe her ego concepts, using the situation as a mirror.

Every situation in life mirrors our ego concepts, but do we have the courage to look in this mirror? As a child, I read the book "The Never Ending Story" by Michael Ende. The hero, Atreyu, had to stand several trials. As he was approaching one of them I remember thinking "What is it going to be? Facing a lion? Fighting a Dragon?" I was deeply disappointed when I found that his challenge was seeing himself in the mirror. Was that really all? No fighting? No glory? I was a child and did not understand that the most terrifying and courageous deed one could be faced with is really seeing oneself in the mirror, stripped of masks and covers. Along our growth process, we face ourselves, and identify the mental components of which we are made. This is bound to be very uncomfortable, and is one of the main reasons why people turn back and shy away from the psychological and spiritual path.

And yet, as you grow while observing the elements of which your self is made up, you are likely to reach a point where you will find it very hard to go back. At difficult moments, my clients frequently tell me that they wish they had not looked in the mirror in the first place, but walking that challenging path now almost seems inevitable. The more you learn about your self and the illusions you once had about it, the harder it is to turn back. At certain moments you may think that ignorance is indeed bliss. There is truth in this. Facing your self and slowly taking apart your ego concepts, and letting go of them and of the self they had created can be a painful process. Letting go of ideas that sustained your psychological self for many years is not easy, but it is the only way to get in touch with who you truly are.

The neutrality of life

The things that irritate you, make you happy or sadden you do not exist in life as it is. These are *your* interpretations of the situation as structured by your ego concepts. The moments themselves are neutral, and do not carry any positive or negative weight. Unfortunately, we rarely keep the moments as they are, and immediately go on to attribute to them our opinions, ideas, and ego concepts.

We build mental stories around reality as it is:

- Reality as it is: I have £120 left
Mental story: I'm broke, I'm a failure
- Reality as it is: The girl refused to give me her phone number
Mental story: I'm ugly; no one will ever want me
Remember: the situations themselves are all neutral.

Weekly exercise 5: This situation was neutral

This exercise aims to develop your sensitivity to events in your life that throw you off balance, and bring to your attention the reasons that cause this. The present exercise is meant to help you notice the effects of your ego concepts: the influence they have on you, and their way of reshaping moments that were originally neutral. It is important for you to realise that your own ego concepts (beliefs, expectations, desires, etc.) were the reason why you interpreted certain moments the way you did.

Whenever a significant event happens, tell yourself:

"This situation was neutral.

I felt _____ (irritated/ angry/ happy/ frustrated/ anything else)

because I _____ (expect.../ want.../ need.../ am afraid of.../ see him/her as.../ anything else...)"

In the second phrase you insert the feeling that accompanied the situation while it was unfolding; the third phrase uncovers the ego concept behind that feeling. Be specific when you note down what it was that you expected/needed/were afraid of, etc. Try this exercise right now: Recall last week and write down a meaningful situation to which you may wish to apply this exercise. At this stage I recommend you focus on situations that had a significant emotional impact on you. This will make it easier to detect the ego concept as well as your emotional response, that is, your interpretation of the moment.

Example:
Situation: I bought a new pair of sunglasses and none of my colleagues at the office noticed them when I walked in this morning.

"This situation was neutral.

I felt [offended and hurt]

because I [need people's attention]

Think of a situation, describe it, and complete the sentence:

The situation:_____

"This situation was neutral.

I felt _____

because I _____

Starting today, keep close track of each of your days. Note down events/experiences/situations that awakened certain feelings, and identify the ego concept that triggered them. Do this every day for a week. Learn the structure by heart: "This situation was neutral. I felt... because I..." Keep repeating this formula as events occur during the day. At the end of the day (or preferably immediately after the event), enter into your learning log the full formula describing two or three events you thought were most significant. As you go on practicing this exercise regularly, you will notice that the feelings you experience during the day are not generated randomly, and that ego concepts clash with the moment and give rise to those feelings. Many of us feel helpless observing our moods and feelings come and go in a manner that seems completely random to an unaware person. Understanding the connection between your feelings and the ego concepts that generate them would give you a wonderful sense of knowledge and self-awareness.

If you practice this exercise regularly for a whole week, you will discover that you are able to notice this pattern even in more subtle circumstances. You will be able to notice ego concepts that interfere with neutral moments and observe the response they provoke in you even when it is not powerful. Keep practicing, and you will realise that this exercise applies to any moment in which your mind reacts to an ongoing event.

By repeating this exercise regularly, you will begin to recognise patterns that are governing your reactions to the world. Among them are automatic reactions that you tend to overlook – flares of anger, moments of pain, emerging fear, powerful anticipation, deep disappointment, and many others that occur when you interact with certain people or engage in certain activities. Most of these reactions occur in patterns that are repeated time and again. You have reached a point where the reaction is automatic and you take it for granted. Therefore you no longer notice it, but this is not unavoidable. In order to break the pattern you should be able to identify it by focusing your attention on the root of the reaction (the ego concept) and its impact. As you practice this exercise for a week with different people and under different circumstances, the fog that blurs your motives will lift, and you will see the source of your attitudes and reactions. Little by little, you will be able to observe your reaction even *before* it kicks in. The ability to recognise an ego concept go into action even before you react is remarkable, as it offers you the choice not to let it take control of your reaction. This is a great step towards freedom.

Choice

My students frequently ask me whether living without ego concepts is at all possible, and how letting go of each and every ego concept would feel. This question misses the point of this work. At this stage, we are not discussing the experience of living without any ego concepts but the idea of *having a choice*. Right now, an ego concept intervenes, pulls you away from the experience as it is, and provokes a reaction. The entire process is automatic. You have no say in it. By practicing the weekly exercises regularly, your relationship with your ego concepts will slowly shift. Instead of catching you unawares, interfering with your life and influencing it, they will become a part of you that you can observe and recognise. Recognition offers you a choice, and when you have a choice you are no longer enslaved to these patterns. Recognition allows you to observe non-reactively, as discussed in lesson 3. Admittedly, this takes time and dedication, but if you truly devote yourself to the practice you will eventually realise that you are able to recognise the process while it is in progress. Imagine that your partner is doing something that has infuriated you in the past. If you practice the exercise regularly, you will be able to notice how this action flares up your anger. You will be able to see this *as it happens* and after a while *before it happens*. By this I mean that you will be able to notice that your partner is doing something that conflicts with your expectations and needs (the ego concept), and you will have the choice to decide whether or not you wish to allow this particular ego concept to dictate what will follow.

This brings us to an important point: Although the situation and your partner's actions are neutral and it is your own needs that are making them seem "wrong", this does not mean that you must automatically accept them. If you notice that a person or a situation is wrong for you – you can choose to let go of it and move on. Notice, though, the great change that has occurred: in the past you would have blamed that person/situation, assuming that something was wrong with them. Now you understand that the perception that those persons or situations are problematic stems from your own ego concepts. You are now able to make a conscious choice. Working with your ego concept, you can decide whether to stay or leave. Once you are able to discern that it is your own perception that makes you feel the way you do, you will learn to take responsibility. You will have a choice.

Psychological measurement 5: Perceived autonomy in life domains scale

In psychological research, choice is measured by means of the concept of autonomy. The perceived autonomy in life domains scale[28] was developed to assess the level of autonomy, i.e. choice, in one's life. It would allow you to examine the levels of choice you experience as you engage with different aspects of life.

Instructions: Please indicate to what extent you agree with each of the following items.

1	Do not agree at all
2	
3	Slightly agree
4	
5	Moderately agree
6	
7	Strongly agree

1	In general, I feel free to do what I want	
2	I have to force myself to act a certain way with people	
3	I do the leisure activities I choose to do	
4	I generally do things because I want to, not because I have to	
5	I feel free to act as I please with other people	
6	The leisure activities I do really correspond to my choices and interests	
7	I feel a freedom of action in my daily activities	

8	I feel free to express myself as I please with other people	
9	I feel I can really do what I want in my leisure activities	
10	I usually feel free to make my own decisions	
11	I feel choked when I am with other people	
12	When I do my leisure activities, I feel I should probably be doing something else	

Scoring: Scale scores are obtained by reversing the scores (1=7, 7=1, 2=6, 6=2, 3=5, 5=3, 4=4) on items 2, 11, and 12 and then summing up all 12 items. Higher scores stand for higher levels of autonomy and choice.

Taking responsibility

Having a choice means that you recognise your own responsibility. Realising that your relationship with the moment stems from your own ego concepts changes your relationship with life. For this change to occur you must actually experience it, and regularly practice making this observation in order to link between your ego concept and your ensuing interpretation of the situation. Once you stop looking for external causes and realise that you are the source of your experiences, you begin taking responsibility for them. The yoga student, who misunderstood the teacher, could point her finger at the teacher and gain nothing, or she could take responsibility and recognise her mind pattern and become aware of her own ego concepts of inferiority. You may ask: "What if the teacher actually meant to insult her?

What if the person who made me uncomfortable really meant for this to happen?" In fact, what really matters is not whether the yoga teacher was being malicious or addressed the student innocently. The reaction (feeling hurt, for example) was triggered *only* because the student had an ego concept that was uncomfortable with who she was. If the student had been completely free of any inferiority-based ego concepts, then she would have simply smiled and continued to practice, no matter what the yoga teacher had meant, or she could have chosen to move on and leave the class. No reaction would have ensued because in order to set off a reaction a mind pattern had to exist that resisted the situation, and was in conflict with it.

Taking responsibility *does not* mean blaming oneself. Blame is just another ego concept. The mind, being in the habit of reacting automatically with an ego concept to any situation, frequently triggers another ego concept, that of guilt: "Oh, I shouldn't judge!" or "This is so wrong, why do I expect that from him?" We are so accustomed to ego-concept-based-reactions that they easily sneak in through the back door.

By switching over from an external point of view (blaming others) to an internal one (recognising your own ego concept) you will be gaining a great benefit: *you* will be in control of the situation. As long as you blame someone or something else and hold them responsible, you can do absolutely nothing about the situation. No matter how hard you try, you will not succeed in changing the situation because the other person might not agree to make the change. This is the beginning of one of the most destructive processes in human relationships: trying to change others to suit our own understanding of the world, our own schemas. Whenever a certain situation conflicts with our schemas, we automatically attempt to reshape the situation in order to be comfortable again. Instead of letting go of the schema, we try to change the world to agree with it. This is where the idea of choice becomes very relevant; as we closely observe ourselves we realise that we can really choose between letting go of the schema (and accepting the situation as it is) or holding on to the schema but moving on and letting go of the situation that makes us uncomfortable. As long as certain situations are in conflict with our schemas, clashes are bound to happen.

Your schemas determine your motivations, whether you are aware of it or not. If something that happens in your life takes you by surprise, you are probably watching a motivation you were unaware of. Remember, an apple tree does not grow pears. If you see pears in the field of your consciousness, you are probably nurturing a pear tree. Most of us live in ignorance, that is, unaware of the seeds, the motivations, which we keep planting with our personal schemas. Taking responsibility means recognising the seeds we plant and realising that the fruit we eat, our experience, is a direct outcome of that original planting.

Opportunity

The idea that our life reflects the ego concepts that make us who we are explains why both difficulty and uplifting experiences can be great opportunities in our growth journey. In the most difficult or joyful moments, a powerful ego concept could be in waiting behind our pain or happiness. When we are overwhelmed by feelings of this kind it is hard to remain observant, to search for an underlying mind pattern that is triggering the emotional response. But that is the most important moment to observe. That is the moment in which a fundamental and powerful pattern is steering our reaction and we must become aware of it, befriend it, and set out on the journey that will enable us to withstand it. That journey begins when you first find the courage and strength to observe your self. The exercises provided in this lesson offer you a clear and practical way to do that.

Lesson 6: The art of presence and meditation techniques

Being present

The art of presence is a fundamental idea of spirituality. This term is frequently used in spiritual jargon and must be fully understood. As mentioned earlier, most of the time we are away from the actual experience, from the moment. Whatever activity we are engaged in, our mind tends to wander and in fact takes us somewhere else. This is where presence becomes relevant. Being present means being fully connected to whatever you do, bringing one hundred percent of your attention and concentration to the experience. Your ego concepts are in the habit of taking over your awareness, and have the power to pull your attention away from the experience and prompt a thought pattern. When your attention is fully focused on the moment, on what is actually happening, no space is left for your ego concepts to interfere with the experience. Through meditation, you have acquired the ability to be present, and your thoughts and expectations no longer divert your attention, which now stays wholly with the experience. Imagine having a conversation with a friend, and note that during much of your communication you are actually not present. When another person speaks we rarely give the speaker our full attention. We think about the next thing we are going to say, we imagine possible responses, we estimate the time needed for them, or even think about dinner. The practice of meditation may not altogether stop certain ego concepts from interfering with the conversation, but it does help you keep your attention focused and not let it drift to the thoughts that have been triggered. Presence, therefore, means being all there, bringing all of your awareness to the experience. That would stand for a meditative communication. The art of presence is a meditative experience you can practice with any kind of activity.

Experimenting with activities into which we normally bring very little awareness is particularly interesting. Take walking, for example. We usually see walking as a means to an end. The only thing that matters is the end point – arriving. The actual experience of walking is disregarded, and consequently we are rarely present when we walk; we think of our plans, worries, expectations, and the place we are heading for. For thousands of years, Buddhist monks in monasteries have practiced the walking meditation technique. For most of us it is a convenient technique because walking is something people experience frequently, and could therefore be an invitation to meditate regularly. In walking meditation we use walking as our focal point, our anchor for attention. To practice this technique, walk slowly and bring your full awareness to your moving body.

Here and now exercise 6: Walking meditation

Next time you walk – at home or outside – practice the walking meditation. When you begin to walk, breathe deeply and imagine the air penetrating as far as your feet and keep your attention focused on your soles. Let your awareness stay with the continuous up and down movement of your feet. Notice first your heel making contact with the ground, and the way the rest of your foot reaches forward all the way to your toes, and then lifts up again and moves in the air. Let your awareness spread to your legs and thighs, observe the way your skin touches your clothes, the temperature, the texture, any sensation you recognise. If you find your mind has wandered, immediately bring your attention back to your feet and legs, smilingly.

Being and thinking

A distinction must be made between two possible relationships with the moment: being and thinking. *Being* in the moment refers to the present, while *thinking* about the moment refers to the past or the future. Any interpretation of the moment is based upon an ego concept that involves by definition past experiences or future expectations. Imagine jumping into the ocean. If you are simply there, soaking in the water and feeling its wetness and temperature, you are *being*. If, on the other hand, your mind starts reacting to the moment by producing ego-concept-based thoughts such as "this is the perfect time of the year to swim in the ocean", then you are not *being*, you are *thinking*. The authentic relationship with life offered by spirituality is essentially a meditative state of being. It invites us to be present in the moment while it unfolds, here and now.

Meditation permeates life

Meditation slowly permeates your everyday life. We frequently think of meditation as a practice that lasts for a determined length of time, and is confined to the specific time of the meditative practice – mornings and evenings, for example. But meditation is not an isolated island in your life, it is the ocean itself. If you practice regularly and observe yourself closely, you will notice how the skill you have been mastering in your meditation sessions slowly makes its way into your other activities. You will be more present when you prepare a report, meet a client, study for an exam, have sex, or communicate with a friend. During each of your activities, you will gradually notice that you are increasingly able to focus your awareness on the actual experience and not let it be diverted by the constant mental noise your mind produces. Closely watch your relationship with the moment: it is an indicator of the impact of meditation on your life. These glimpses of your newly-acquired presence are very important; they are the meeting points between your daily practice of meditation and your experience of life as a continuous meditative state. No matter which specific meditation technique you practice, it is a gateway to presence.

Psychological research: Mind-wandering

Psychological research carried out in this area explores the experience of presence which is the equivalent of being mindful. When you are mindful you are aware of the experience, of the moment, and fully attend to it. These are the times when your mind does not wander; it is fully focused on the event unfolding in the moment. A fascinating study evaluating the wandering mind and presence was published under the title "A Wandering Mind is an Unhappy Mind"[29]. The researchers developed a web application for mobile phones that allowed them to recruit over 15,000 participants and compiling a large database. With this application, the participants were contacted randomly during their waking hours, and were given a number of questions. The first question was a happiness question: "How are you feeling right now?" and the answer could range from 0 (very bad) to 100 (very good). The second question was an activity question: "What are you doing right now?" and the participant had to choose one or several of 22 daily activities such as working, conversing, preparing food, and commuting. The third and final question was "Are you thinking about something other than what you are currently doing?" and the participant had to choose between one of the following four options: 1. No (which means that there was no mind-wandering, they were present, mindful) 2. Yes, thinking about something pleasant 3. Yes, thinking about something neutral 4. Yes, thinking about something unpleasant. Options 2-4 stood for mind-wandering, specifically indicating whether the participant's mind wandered to something pleasant, neutral, or unpleasant. The data collected this way provided the researchers with the information required to find out whether there is any link between mindfulness and wellbeing. The results were unequivocal: People reported higher levels of happiness when they were present and mindful than in moments of mind-wandering. You may be thinking "sure, on average, but what if their minds wandered to something pleasant?" The researchers compared being mindful to each of the three mind-wandering options and found that being mindful produced higher levels of happiness than any of them. The greatest gap was found between being mindful and thinking about something unpleasant, a smaller gap was found between being mindful and thinking about something natural, and the smallest – between being mindful and thinking about something pleasant; and yet the gap was always in favour of being mindful. The author of the research compared mind wandering to playing slot machines where in one you always lose $10, in the other $5, and the final one $1; why would you choose to play if you know you cannot win? This is another example of the support spiritual concepts and ideas get from contemporary psychological research. The idea of being "here and now" appears in countless spiritual texts, and is consistently accompanied by emphasis on the importance of meditation as the tool to achieve presence, and its benefits to our wellbeing. We now have an abundance of psychological studies, such as the one described above, validating an area that once appeared to be "out of bounds" for the scientific community, and making it increasingly accepted.

Psychological measurement 6: Mindfulness questionnaire

An important aspect of psychological research involves measuring the levels of mindful attention to evaluate the psychological impact of mindfulness. A variety of assessment tools (mostly questionnaires) have been put together in order to measure the extent of an individual's awareness, and find out whether that individual is attending to whatever is taking place at a given moment. An example of such an assessment tool is the Five Facet Mindfulness Questionnaire (FFMQ)[30].

Instructions: Please rate each of the following statements using the scale provided. Write the number that best describes your own opinion of what is generally true for you.

1	Never or vary rarely true
2	Rarely true
3	Sometimes true
4	Often true
5	Very often or always true

1	When I'm walking, I deliberately notice the sensations of my body moving.	
2	I'm good at finding words to describe my feelings.	
3	I criticize myself for having irrational or inappropriate emotions.	
4	I perceive my feelings and emotions without having to react to them.	
5	When I do things, my mind wanders off and I'm easily distracted.	
6	When I take a shower or bath, I stay alert to the sensations of water on my body.	
7	I can easily put my beliefs, opinions, and expectations into words.	

8	I don't pay attention to what I'm doing because I'm daydreaming, worrying, or otherwise distracted.	
9	I watch my feelings without getting lost in them.	
10	I tell myself I shouldn't be feeling the way I'm feeling.	
11	I notice how foods and drinks affect my thoughts, bodily sensations, and emotions.	
12	It's hard for me to find the words to describe what I'm thinking.	
13	I am easily distracted.	
14	I believe some of my thoughts are abnormal or bad and I shouldn't think that way.	
15	I pay attention to sensations, such as the wind in my hair or sun on my face.	
16	I have trouble thinking of the right words to express how I feel about things.	
17	I make judgments about whether my thoughts are good or bad.	
18	I find it difficult to stay focused on what's happening in the present.	

19	When I have distressing thoughts or images, I "step back" and am aware of the thought or image without getting taken over by it.	
20	I pay attention to sounds, such as clocks ticking, birds chirping, or cars passing.	
21	In difficult situations, I can pause without immediately reacting.	
22	When I have a sensation in my body, it's difficult for me to describe it because I can't find the right words.	
23	It seems I am "running on automatic" without much awareness of what I'm doing.	
24	When I have distressing thoughts or images, I feel calm soon after.	
25	I tell myself that I shouldn't be thinking the way I'm thinking.	
26	I notice the smells and aromas of things.	
27	Even when I'm feeling terribly upset, I can find a way to put it into words.	
28	I rush through activities without being really attentive to them.	

29	When I have distressing thoughts or images I am able just to notice them without reacting.	
30	I think some of my emotions are bad or inappropriate and I shouldn't feel them.	
31	I notice visual elements in art or nature, such as colors, shapes, textures, or patterns of light and shadow.	
32	My natural tendency is to put my experiences into words.	
33	When I have distressing thoughts or images, I just notice them and let them go.	
34	I do jobs or tasks automatically without being aware of what I'm doing.	
35	When I have distressing thoughts or images, I judge myself as good or bad, depending what the thought/image is about.	
36	I pay attention to how my emotions affect my thoughts and behavior.	
37	I can usually describe how I feel at the moment in considerable detail.	
38	I find myself doing things without paying attention.	
39	I disapprove of myself when I have irrational ideas.	

Scoring: The scale is made out of five subscales. For each subscale, sum the scores of the appropriate items. Higher scores stand for higher levels of mindfulness in that subscale. For all items marked "R" the scoring must be reversed (1=5, 5=1, 2=4, 4=2, 3=3).

Observing: Do you observe sensations and emotions in your body?

1, 6, 11, 15, 20, 26, 31, 36

Describing: Can you easily describe experiences you are aware of?

2, 7, 12R, 16R, 22R, 27, 32, 37

Acting with Awareness: Are you mindful when you act?

5R, 8R, 13R, 18R, 23R, 28R, 34R, 38R

Non-Judging of inner experience: Are you accepting your inner experiences?

3R, 10R, 14R, 17R, 25R, 30R, 35R, 39R

Non-reactivity to inner experience: Are you reacting to your inner-experience?

4, 9, 19, 21, 24, 29, 33

Meditation techniques

When meditation is being discussed, the first image that comes to mind is someone sitting rigidly, eyes closed, focusing on breath. Indeed, this meditation technique is very popular, but there are hundreds of other techniques that may prove to be as useful for you. Every meditation technique has its unique characteristics, and invites you to experience meditation in a different way. They all invite you to direct your attention at one focal point, but these focal points may be essentially different. Each meditation technique provides a unique focal point that delivers a distinctive invitation; your willingness to accept the invitation you are offered depends on the way you experience it, and the extent to which you are comfortable with it. The next section brings a description of some well known and commonly used meditation techniques. Among them you will probably find one or several that best suit your particular personality, and which you will be comfortable practicing.

Breathing meditations: In lesson 2, we described and practiced the classic approach to breathing meditation. Yet breathing is also incorporated into various other meditation techniques. Because breathing is highly effective as an attention anchor, many meditation techniques suggest hooking your attention to your breath and letting it ride it as part of meditation. For example, several body-scanning meditations (discussed below) invite you to direct your attention at your inner body; these techniques often use breath as a vehicle that drives your attention through different parts of the body, and steers your awareness from one part to the other. In other words, breathing helps prevent your awareness from being carried away by your thoughts while you meditate. To practice the classic breathing meditation, repeat Weekly exercise 2.

Imagery/Visual meditations: In an imagery meditation your focal point, your anchor, is an image. Certain religions use images of their deities as their focal points, but any image that invites your attention to fully attend to it is a good choice. You may visualise a seascape or a landscape, for example. Another visual meditation technique is focusing on an actual object rather than on a visualized one. In this case you keep your eyes open and focus your attention on an object placed in front of you. A burning candle is often used as a focal point in visual meditation, but you can equally direct your attention at a vase or a flower. Because you keep your eyes open during the practice you may consider trying it in public places. Whenever you sit in a waiting room or take a train, simply pick up any object in front of you and meditate. The beauty of this simple meditation is that after a while, and with some practice, you will find it can be done anytime and anywhere. To practice it, first choose an object, then sit comfortably, keep your eyes open, and focus your full attention on the colours, texture, and shape of that object. Try keeping your attention fully focused on the object for ten minutes. If you find that your mind has wandered, immediately return your attention to the object, smilingly.

Auditory meditations: Some people find music enchanting. Its sound is so captivating that everything else disappears and they are completely immersed in it. If you are one of these people, perhaps auditory meditation will come most naturally to you. In auditory meditations you bring your full attention to sound. The sound of the waves, or sounds made by dolphins or whales are the best known examples, but any music that captivates your attention is appropriate. The music you choose as your focal point must be without lyrics (chanting is an exception, as will be discussed later), to avoid feeding the mind with thinking material. The combination of music and lyrics would add difficulty to maintaining your focus, as your mind will keep reacting to the ideas of the text. To exercise an auditory meditation, put on a certain soundtrack or a piece of music. Sit comfortably, close your eyes, and focus all your attention on the music. Focus on the sound, the changing beats, new instruments that come in and fade away, and moments of silence; allow your awareness to be completely absorbed in the music for ten minutes. If you find that your mind has wandered, immediately bring your attention back to the music, smilingly.

Verbal meditations: Certain branches of spirituality maintain that words carry energy in varying intensity, and that carefully chosen words can be used as focal points. Hinduism and Buddhism have sacred words or sounds that are repeated during prayer, meditation, or chanting. A word or a sound of this kind is called a Mantra. If the idea of a Mantra makes you uncomfortable, think about it as another kind of object to bring your attention to. In Transcendental Meditation (TM), a popular meditation technique, individual meditators are given particular Mantras thought to be appropriate for them, and are asked to stay completely focused on the Mantra while they meditate.

Another technique that combines auditory and verbal meditations is that of chanting, in which the meditators incorporate a series of Mantras into their chanting. To exercise this meditation, think of a single word that is meaningful for you, for example, the word "water". Sit comfortably, close your eyes, and repeat the word "water" in your mind slowly, over and over again. Focus every bit of your attention on the word. Allow your awareness to be completely absorbed in the word for ten minutes. If you find that your mind has wandered immediately bring your attention back to the word, smilingly.

Active meditations: This technique includes a variety of meditations during which you are active, in movement. For many people, meditating in an immobile posture is uncomfortable. But you do not have to sit still in order to meditate. Practicing meditation with your attention focused on your moving body is beautiful. The classic example of an active meditation technique is the walking meditation you practiced earlier. Another branch of active meditation was invented by the Indian spiritual teacher Osho. Most of his meditations take 60 minutes and comprise a number of stages. The first few stages are usually more active while the final stages tend to be more relaxed and calm. Osho claimed that the ancient sitting-breathing meditation was created thousands of years ago for the people who lived in those times. In our days, he says, the pace and challenges of life are so different that this type of meditation is less applicable, and active meditation techniques may prove more relevant. If you wish to try a number of these meditations, search for Osho's active "Kundalini meditation" and "Dynamic meditation" guidelines.

Another example of active meditation you could explore is that of the "Five Rhythms", devised by Gabrielle Roth. This technique takes the body and the mind through a five-stage meditative experience that moves through Flowing, Staccato, Chaos, Lyrical, and ends with Stillness. A similar movement meditation is the "Biodanza", created by Rolando Toro, which is another invitation for the body to move freely to the sound of music and connect to one's emotions. This develops awareness to whatever is moving within you during the dance. Yoga, as originally intended, is an active meditation. In yoga your body experiences the asana (the posture) in a way that is expected to create space in your body, into which you bring your awareness. During a yoga session your whole body becomes receptive, invites your breath, grips your awareness, and therefore keeps your attention fully focused and in the moment, in the movement of the body. Another remarkable active meditation is the Sufi whirling meditation. One Sufi faction, known as the Whirling Dervishes, transcends the analytic activity of the mind and meditates by means of a spinning dance, followed by a period of contemplation. They spread their arms, one palm facing the sky and the other facing the ground, gaze into the horizon, and whirl, keeping their attention on the sensation of whirling.

All these meditative experiences share the idea that the movement of your body can be a wonderful focal point for meditation. To exercise this type of meditation, find a room where you have some space to move. Choose music that encourages you to move freely, but not necessarily fast-beat music; on the contrary, you may begin by choosing slower music, to help you keep your attention on the movements of the body. You may feel slightly self-conscious or embarrassed at first; remind yourself that you are alone in the room, and no one is watching or judging you. Allow yourself to move freely. In this meditation, the way you move is not prescribed. Let your body move at any rhythm and way you feel is right at that moment. You may find yourself dancing around the room, and you may stand in one place moving ever so slightly. A few minutes into the practice you may discover that you wish to make broader movements or change the rhythm. It is best to begin the meditation with small and slow movements in order to get the feel of your body before you move on to more expansive movements. Let your awareness be completely absorbed in the movement of your body for ten minutes. If your arms slowly rise on both sides of your body, focus on their movement, the feeling in the muscles, the way the chest opens, and any other bodily sensation. If you are moving your hips, focus your attention on that area, observe your legs and see if they are involved; if they are – direct your awareness at them. The important point is that you stay in tune, connected with your body, and aware of its movements. If you find that your mind has wandered, immediately bring your attention back to the movement of the body, smilingly.

Mindfulness: Mindfulness meditation involves observing the feelings, images, sensations, thoughts, smells, sounds that flood your consciousness. The focal point here is your whole consciousness, which is open to receive and take in any kind of stimuli. You do not pursue these stimuli, but wait for them to rise and then disappear. In the course of mindfulness meditation, the meditator consciously watches whatever passes through his body and mind: Any physical sensation or mental activity is noticed without reaction until it dissipates and is replaced by a new one. You become the observer of this rise and fall of stimuli as if you were watching a movie screened in your mind and body. In mindfulness meditation your awareness shifts from one focal point to another, similarly to what happens if your mind is scattered. And yet these are two completely different states of mind. Mindfulness occurs when your awareness is completely absorbed in focal points that belong in the present moment. Stimuli that come and go here and now: from the colour of the wall, to the light of the sun, to the sound of your breath. In contrast, a scattered mind focuses on past and future focal points of the mind that are disconnected from the present moment: from a conversation you had with your boss yesterday, to its future implications for your job, to the idea of leaving your job. Therefore, although they both involve a flowing, moving mind, the experience is fundamentally different: You are fully present in mindfulness and completely disengaged from the here and now with a scattered mind.

Mindfulness meditation is an excellent means to learn the art of non-attachment, discussed in lesson 4. It teaches you how to become aware of an emotion, a sensation, an idea, an image, and then to let them go, without getting attached to any of them. Meditation is not meant to stop you thinking or feeling, but to change your relationship with these thoughts and feelings: If once they seized your attention and prevented you from being present, you now notice them without reaction. A good way to visualize mindfulness meditation is to imagine that your consciousness is the sky, and your awareness is fully focused on it. You will notice thoughts and feelings drift by like clouds in the sky of your consciousness. Normally, these clouds would lead to a series of internal reactions. Some days will be stormy and windy, with many clouds passing by chaotically; other days will be more peaceful, with fewer and slower clouds passing by. No matter what your internal weather is, in mindfulness meditation your task is to notice the sensation, thought, or emotion, and allow them to dissipate naturally, with no reaction at all.

To exercise this meditation technique, sit straight in front of a wall and allow your eyelids to relax so that your eyes are not tightly closed but remain half open. Now simply observe whatever is happening. Do nothing but noticing any sensations, feelings, thoughts, or images that pass through your mind, without becoming involved with any of them. If you do not react to a sensation or thought, it will rise and fall and then disappear. You could describe in your mind what you are noticing: "heat", "tightening in chest", "thinking of boredom", "seeing an image of a bird", etc. You may discover that different sensations, thoughts or feelings occur simultaneously; if this happens, choose one stimulus and keep your awareness with it until it disappears, then observe the next stimulus. Allow your awareness to be completely absorbed in whatever it is that you notice – without reacting – for ten minutes. If you find that your mind has wandered, triggering a chain of reactive thoughts, immediately bring your attention back smilingly, and continue watching the open sky of your consciousness.

Body scanning meditations: The body is a wonderful focal point for your awareness. Body scanning meditation techniques invite your attention to move through your body, focus on different parts, and notice what is happening in these areas. Unlike active meditations, during which your body is in motion, you remain immobile during body-scanning meditations. You can lie down, sit, or stand; try each of the three postures to determine which of them suits you best when you practice this technique. Any meditation that involves conscious scanning of your body in a non-analytical way is a body-scanning technique. In practicing this meditation you will use your breath as a vehicle for guiding your attention into different parts of the body. Start at your feet and move up slowly to the top of your head. When you reach the top of the head – move back slowly to your feet. Repeat this scan until your meditation time is up; if you have no time restrictions, simply continue until you feel that it is time to open your eyes. The following instructions will help you use your breath to bring your awareness into the particular area on which you are focusing: Remain in each area for the length of two breaths before you move on. Begin the practice by breathing deeply and bringing your awareness to your feet. Focus your attention on your feet and mentally observe that area. Move up to your ankles and then drive your awareness through your shins and into your knees. Focus on your thighs and then your hips. Scan your back without hurry. Begin at your lower back, move up to the middle back, and end with the upper back. Breathe into your shoulders, gradually slide into your elbows, then into your lower arms and finally bring your awareness to the palms of your hands. Breathe into your neck, your face, your scalp, and the top of your head. Now move your awareness back along the same route. It does not matter if you miss some parts; just scan most of your body from your feet to the top of the head and back. For ten minutes, keep your full attention on your bodily sensations at each scanned area; if your mind has wandered immediately bring your attention back to that particular body area, smilingly.

Love-compassion-acceptance meditations: This branch of meditation techniques deepens one's awareness in a manner that enhances unconditional love, acceptance, and compassion. This is the undercurrent flowing within the Authentic Self, and these meditation techniques invite us to swim in this river of unconditional love that lies within us. A popular example of these techniques is the Loving-Kindness Meditation (LKM). Unlike mindfulness meditation, where we focus our awareness on the present in an open-minded and non-judgemental manner, LKM encourages us to focus our awareness on warm tender feelings, open-heartedly. A study by Fredrickson and her colleagues[31] gave a seven-week workshop of LKM meditation to 140 participants. Practicing the LKM for the duration of the workshop increased the participants' levels of positive emotions such as gratitude, hope, pride, contentment and love, while creating a stronger feeling of satisfaction with life. To practice the LKM follow the instructions below:

- **Sit comfortably. Any position will do.** Close your eyes and take a few deep breaths. Inhale and exhale slowly, and consciously relax your muscles and prepare body and mind for deep awareness of love and compassion.
- **Choose a person you love.** Choose someone who you love easily and naturally rather than someone for whom you feel an emotionally complicated love.
- **Focus on the area around your heart.** Put your hand over your heart. Once you are able to focus on your heart, imagine breathing in and out through your heart. Take several deep breaths and feel your heart breathing.
- **Turn your attention to feelings of gratitude and love,** warm and tender feelings, for the person you chose.
- **Send loving-kindness and compassion to yourself:** Imagine that the warm glow of love and compassion coming from your heart is moving throughout your body. Send these feelings up and down your body. If verbal content is easier for you to connect to, you can repeat the following words: May I be happy. May I be well. May I be safe. May I be peaceful and at ease.
- **Send loving-kindness and compassion to family and friends:** Imagine friends and family as vividly as you can, and send these feelings into their hearts. Imagine the warm glow of love and compassion that comes from your heart moving into their hearts. If verbal content is easier for you to connect to, you can repeat the following words: May you be happy. May you be well. May you be safe. May you be peaceful and at ease.
- **Expand the circle** by sending your loving-kindness and compassion to neighbours, acquaintances, strangers, animals, and finally people with whom you have difficulty.
- **Imagine planet earth, with all of its inhabitants,** and send loving-kindness and compassion to all living beings.
- **For ten minutes**, keep your full attention on the sensations

and feelings of loving-kindness and compassion. If your awareness has wandered immediately bring back your attention to those tender and warm feelings, smilingly.

Changing techniques

Some of my students tell me that they are unable to meditate, and that they find meditation too uncomfortable. They have tried it for weeks on end, they say, to no avail. I advise these people to try a different technique. For example, if they have been practicing the sitting and breathing meditation for weeks, and found it brought them nowhere, I may advise them to try the walking meditation for a few weeks. The results are often astonishing. Suddenly meditation becomes doable; of course, they may still face difficulties on certain days, but the experience now appears simpler and more natural. Why? Because they have finally found the meditation that is right *for them*. No meditation technique is right for everyone. If your personal strength lies in visualisation, you may find it easier to meditate by focusing on an image. If you love moving and dancing, active meditation may come more naturally to you. Matching the meditation technique to your strength areas would be wise. At the beginning of the process, I advise you to choose a meditation technique that you find simple and natural. This is an important but rarely discussed aspect of meditation: Meditation techniques are extremely versatile and you should find the one that is right for you. Imagine you go out with someone and after a few dates you feel that this person is not right for you. Would you abandon romantic relationships altogether? Of course not, you would search for the one that feels natural and right. It does not have to be easy (frequently it is not) but it must feel right. The search for the right meditation technique may not be easy, but it is highly rewarding.

Having found a technique that suits you does not mean you should reject all the others. With time, we change and grow. You may find that different meditation techniques are particularly effective at specific points in your life, and maximise your growth potential. It is therefore important to remain open to the call of change. It is easy to get comfortable with a certain meditation technique and forget about all the rest. Having a friendly meditation technique that you can go back to at any point in time is important, but you must also be open to other techniques. There is no guarantee that a meditation technique which is appropriate today will be relevant tomorrow.

Weekly exercise 6: Meditation techniques

Practice for a week one of the eight meditation techniques described above, for at least ten minutes in the morning and ten minutes in the evening. Choose the technique that suits you best. Once you have completed a week of a certain meditation technique, you may explore any of the other ones by practicing them for a subsequent week. Use the following table to monitor your experiences with each meditation technique:

Meditation technique	Morning/ evening/ both	Length of session	Experience of meditation	Effect of meditation

Under *"Meditation"* write the name of the practiced meditation technique.

Under *"Morning/evening/both"* write whether you practiced it in the morning, in the evening, or in both.

Under *"Length of time"* write the total time you dedicated to practicing this meditation.

Under *"Experience of meditation"* give a short description of your own feelings *during* the meditation. Were you comfortable? Did you feel joy? Irritation? Impatience? Were you at peace?

Under *"Effect of meditation"* give a short description of your feelings *after* the meditation. How did you feel on that day or evening? What impact, if at all, did the meditation have on your day or evening? What influence did it have on your other experiences? On the way you communicated with others? On the way you approached difficulties and challenges?

Meditation will not make you passive

Students frequently tell me they fear that regular practice of meditation will make them sit passively, never moving anywhere. They are worried that meditation could detach them from life as they once knew it. In reality, the only thing meditation detaches you from is your ego concepts, that is, your *interpretation* of life. Getting detached from one's ego concepts means *connecting* with life. As a result of meditation you are thrown into *life as it is*. The main issue here is avoiding automaticity. When you allow meditation to slowly penetrate into your way of being, you gradually stop reacting automatically to life. Automatic reactions prompted by your ego concepts no longer occupy space in your awareness and therefore you experience choice. That is exactly what I mean when I say Awareness Is Freedom: You become aware of the potential of each moment and stop reacting automatically out of your ego concepts. Remember, the task of ego concepts is to make sure you are safe, secure, within your comfort zone. But life has so much more to offer, so many potential paths that are only revealed when the ego concept blinkers are removed.

Meditation, therefore, does not work against life, it is rather life supporting; it takes the blinkers away and allows you to truly see whatever stands in front of you. This is crucial because that is the space where life's opportunities lie. Many people believe that no opportunities are available to them simply because they have been conditioned for so many years to observe life via the filter of their ego concepts. This filter allows you to see only the safe options, those that are within your comfort zone, and it is not surprising you may find life dull, grey, and meaningless. How could life be exciting and vibrant if its juice has been squeezed away by the filtering process? Meditation creates a new inner space within which you can act and make choices. You are no longer a leaf in the wind, tossed around by your reactions to your ego concepts; now you become the wind, you can choose and navigate consciously because you set out from a calm and centred space within you.

Developing Meditation

Meditation begins by inviting transcendence into the simplest circumstances, such as sitting or breathing by yourself. We begin with this straightforward task because when you begin your meditation practice your mind is so deeply conditioned to fluctuate that the slightest disturbance pulls your attention away, into the whirlwind of thought. As you practice and become more experienced you will find that you can perform increasingly complex tasks without being thrown out of the meditative state. You begin by sitting down and breathing, then you may meditate while washing the dishes, walking on a busy street, and even if you are not alone in the room. These are more challenging forms of meditation as they require that you ignore many stimuli that are able to distract you or kick-start the thinking mind. By practicing meditation in a less challenging environment, you slowly build up a "meditative resilience" that would allow you to remain centred in more complex situations. The ultimate, perhaps most challenging situation, is remaining present during communication with other people. When we communicate with others we are rarely capable of being present, because the mind is flooded with so many stimuli triggering ego concepts. Osho, the spiritual teacher, used to ask his students to go out and meditate in the market place. Imagine sitting and meditating in the middle of this pandemonium. But there is an important lesson behind his request. Meditation is not meant to be experienced in isolation; it should be an integral part of life. Take meditation retreats, for example. These retreats are important as they allow a glimpse into the meditative state of no-mind and transcendence. Many spiritual teachings recommend spending certain periods of time at retreats, and dedicating them to meditation in order to deepen the meditative experience. Many of these retreats are characterized by silence and sometime solitude. We can easily escape to the high mountains, to a cave, to a monastery – we might even reach an extended state of transcendence in such a place – but it would be an experience achieved under very specific circumstances. It would be similar to meditating alone in a room and claiming that you have mastered meditation. Ultimately, you should be able to achieve transcendence at any moment of life, under any circumstances, whether easy or hard, at sad and happy moments. This is when the meditators leave their retreats, return to "real life", and implement their newly-acquired skill in an environment that confronts them with their deepest ego concepts. The skill of meditation is best applied in moments defined by your mind as difficult and challenging. By developing the skill on your own in a quiet space you slowly build it up in a way that allows you to implement it in more challenging situations. This would probably take time and patience, but you will eventually gather experience with meditation, and naturally develop your meditative skill.

By developing your skills of meditation you will also be able to remain in a meditative non-analytical state for longer periods of time. It is natural to awaken to the moment (be present) and then have it slip away again (become lost in your thoughts), and then awaken and fall asleep again. Enhancing awareness via the meditative experience will shorten the time between each awakening. The meditative skill, as any other skill, develops through practice. When you first practice meditation you may discover that you are unable to focus non-analytically on your breath for more than about 30 seconds out of a ten-minute practice, and that your mind wanders for the other nine and a half minutes, and you will "catch" yourself thinking. That is completely natural. As you practice, your skill of concentration will *gradually* improve and these 30 seconds will extend to 40 and then 50 seconds, until you are able to stay focused on your breath for long minutes without the interruption of thought. This practice might take a long time but every journey begins with a first step.

Consistent and regular practice will result in:

- A steadier meditative state (remaining in meditation for longer periods of time).
- An ability to meditate in complex and challenging situations.

Regular practice will expand your meditative experience in a natural way. You will gradually notice that meditation is touching moments and situations where you have hardly been present in the past. Be attentive to your life and you may find that many of your experiences are influenced by the meditative state in a way that is new and exciting. Our body and mind are extremely flexible and transformable. All you have to do is practice consistently, and let things evolve naturally.

Lesson 7: Impermanence: This Too Shall Pass

Life is change

Impermanence, the certainty that everything changes constantly, is a fundamental law of life. We watch the world around us changing all the time: nature with the seasons, society, and our emotions. And yet, we tend to deny, fight, and reject impermanence. We dislike change. In Lesson 1, we discussed our need to feel safe and secure, and the way this need leads to the creation of our ego concepts. In our discussion of impermanence we delve deeper into this need. Impermanence is the antithesis of the safety we are longing for. Throughout life, we all make efforts to keep our experiences durable and predictable, so that we can remain within our comfort zone. By accepting the very idea of impermanence we resign to the fact that we will eventually lose the battle. No matter how hard we try to hold on to an idea, a partner, a job, or an emotion, the day will come when it will change, shape-shift, or disappear. Although we know that change is inevitable, we refuse to accept it. With zeal and determination we set out to build an impossible life, a life that stands still, does not move and will only stir at our command. But we all know that life is indifferent to our wishes. It has its own rhythm and flow, and is in constant movement that does not seem to have a rational direction or explanation.

Interestingly, you may be nodding your head in agreement at these words, because *intellectually* they make sense. But deep down you do not believe and accept the idea of change; you keep hoping that cherished aspects of your life will remain constant. The unavoidable truth is that your partner, your job, your friends, and almost every other dimension of your life are bound to undergo changes sooner or later. Impermanence is inevitable, even if we find it difficult to accept.

Stress: Psychological reaction to impermanence

Psychological research shows that three parameters determine whether we perceive an event as stressful or not: Controllability, predictability, and the extent to which this event challenges our comfort zone.

The first parameter indicates that the less control we have over an event, the more stressful it is. That is why events that are completely beyond our control, such as death or serious illness, are extremely stressful. In one interesting study[32], two groups of participants were shown photographs of dead bodies to induce stress. The only difference between the groups was that the participants of one group had a button which they could press to make the photograph disappear, while the other group had no such button. In other words, the first group had some control over the stressful event while the second group had none. The results were as predicted: The levels of stress were significantly lower in the participants who had a button to press than in those who did not. Knowing that we are able to control an event makes it less stressful.

The second parameter is predictability, i.e., being able to predict that a stressful event is about to occur reduces the level of stress. A warning signal provides us with time to prepare and come up with a response that could ease the impact of the stressful event. This allows for some confidence that reduces stress.

The third parameter has to do with whether or not the event challenges your limits, whether or not it pushes you out of your comfort zone. The more challenging an event is to your limits, the more stressful it is. If, for example, speaking before an audience is within your comfort zone, then an event of this kind may merely cause slight stress. But if it challenges your limits, you will experience the event as extremely stressful.

Understanding stress is highly relevant to the discussion of impermanence. Impermanence incorporates the perfect elements to create an environment of low controllability and predictability, while challenging your comfort zone. A changing environment is unpredictable and out of control. At some point, a changing environment is bound to create a situation that is beyond your comfort zone. Impermanence, therefore, is daunting. In order to fight it we form as many ego concepts as possible, create an Ego Formed Self, and pad our life with false stability. We all realize that this stability is an illusion; people do go away and get fired, relationships change, and our emotions fluctuate, yet we do everything possible to keep our life as stable as possible.

Impermanence is sensed as dangerous

By relinquishing some of our ego concepts we open up to the impermanence of life, and truly accept it. This is sensed as dangerous, as if anything could happen at any moment; indeed, that is true and challenging at the same time. And yet, when you stop fighting this possibility, when you truly accept impermanence, you end the conflict between the natural course of the unfolding moment and your mind's attempts to harness it and command it to unfold in a steady, safe, and secure way. This is a constant battle that you are rarely aware of, but one that has a powerful emotional impact on you. You carry in your mind specific guidelines and expect life to follow them. Sometimes life does follow them, but at other times it does not. When this happens, your expectations clash with life as it is, creating a deep feeling of discomfort and frustration. As long as we deny impermanence, we invite this discomfort on a regular basis. When we truly accept impermanence, we accept the changes and twists that life throws at us – and the conflict ends. Once the conflict ends, you feel great relief, as if a fight you were not even aware of is suddenly over. Kabat Zinn said: "You can't stop the waves, but you can learn to surf" [34]. Right now we are throwing ourselves at the wave of life, and frequently crash against it.

Surfing means feeling the wave, accepting it, and moving with it, leaving behind our ego concepts.

"It has often been said that the only unchanging thing in the world is change itself. Life is continuously changing, evolving, dying, and being reborn. All opposites play part in this vast circular pattern. If you cling to the edge of the wheel you can get dizzy! Move toward the centre of the cyclone and relax, knowing that this too will pass."
Osho[35]

Psychological measurement 7: Personal Meaning in Life

One of the areas where impermanence is sensed as dangerous is personal meaning in life. Many of us attempt to find personal meaning; knowing our meaning provides us with great vitality, passion, and enthusiasm. However, the danger of finding meaning is the illusion that this is the end of our search; meaning will now remain constant in our lives, without change or movement. This might be our hope, and yet our personal meaning is part of that same never-ending flow of impermanence and change. High levels of awareness are needed in our relationship with personal meaning, to ensure that our current experience of meaning is indeed the authentic and relevant one.

The Meaning in Life Questionnaire (MLQ)[33] was developed to assess the extent to which your life is filled with meaning. The questionnaire is divided into two subscales: Presence of meaning in life (measuring the actual level of meaning in your life) and the Search for meaning in life (measuring the extent to which you search for meaning).

Instructions: Please take a moment to think about what makes your life and existence feel important and significant to you. Please respond to the following statements as truthfully and accurately as you can, and also please remember that these are very subjective questions and that there are no right or wrong answers. For each of the statements below please choose an answer between 1 (Absolutely untrue) and 7 (Absolutely true).

1	Absolutely untrue
2	Moderately untrue
3	Slightly untrue
4	Neither true nor untrue
5	Slightly true
6	Moderately true
7	Absolutely true

1	I understand my life's meaning.	
2	I am looking for something that makes my life feel meaningful.	
3	I am always looking to find my life's purpose.	
4	My life has a clear sense of purpose.	
5	I have a good sense of what makes my life meaningful.	
6	I have discovered a satisfying life purpose.	

7	I am always searching for something that makes my life feel significant.	
8	I am seeking a purpose or mission for my life.	
9	My life has no clear purpose.	
10	I am searching for meaning in my life.	

Scoring: Presence related questions are: 1, 4, 5, 6, & 9-reversed (for question 9 only: 1=7, 7=1, 2=6, 6=2, 3=5, 5=3, 4=4). Search related questions are = 2, 3, 7, 8, & 10. Scores are obtained by summing up the scores of all relevant questions. Higher scores stand for higher levels of presence and search.

Emotional polarity and the authentic self

Impermanence is at the heart of the difference between emotions that depend on and stem from an external event, and the feelings that accompany the enlightened experience. What is the difference between these two? You may think: "I feel love, joy, compassion and peace in my everyday life; am I not enlightened?" There is one crucial difference between emotions experienced in a normal state of consciousness of the Ego Formed Self, and the way we experience them within the undercurrent of our enlightened Authentic Self. Normally, when our mind is in charge, these emotional responses simply indicate that something has been happening that matches our ego concepts' definition of "right" or "wrong". A certain need or expectation is being fulfilled. The ego concept involved may be an expectation that someone would give us attention ("when she or he gives me attention, I feel happy"); once you get this attention you feel joy and satisfaction. This feeling *depends* upon something; it emerges when something happens that meets your mind's requirements. The same applies to peace and relaxation. You have just completed an important task at work, you are given a few days off, and you feel peaceful and relaxed. That peaceful feeling depends upon specific circumstances that correspond to your ego concept ("when I am not burdened by a major responsibility, I feel calm"). The first difficulty, therefore, is that those feelings of happiness and peace are dependent upon an external event. Whether or not you experience this joy and peace is not in your hands.

Another underlying difficulty is that potentially, ego concepts have two polar consequences: If a person indeed gives you the attention you long for, you will feel happy. But what if you get no attention? If the expectations of your ego concepts are not fulfilled, you will find yourself at the other emotional pole; you will be flooded with sadness, suffering, and pain. Not only does your happiness depend on an external factor, it is now walking hand in hand with misery. These poles always go together. If one pole materializes, you may be sure that the other one is lurking behind, and it is only a matter of time before the circumstances are right for it to emerge. Impermanence guarantees that at some point we will be served the dish we detest. For every instance of attention there will be an instance of indifference, or rather what your mind interprets as such. This does not involve only feelings of happiness and sadness. It is true for any other feeling. Take the relaxation and peace you feel when you are temporarily relieved of your responsibilities at work. You know that you will soon find yourself taking responsibility for another important project at work, and immediately begin to struggle with stress and anxiety, which are polar to peace and relaxation.

The cycle of misery

The Buddha named this sequence of events "the cycle of misery": At every moment of your life you are faced with two opposing impulses: craving and rejecting. You either react to an event in your life with craving ("yes, that's great, I want more") or with rejecting ("no, I dislike it, I don't want it"). Obviously, the intensity of craving and rejecting varies, depending on the importance you attach to each event, but the fundamental automatic reaction remains the same. If you take a close look at your cravings and rejections, you will see that they represent a polarity themselves: You crave to have many people around you in order to reject an underlying loneliness.

Your cravings and rejections stem from your particular ego concepts and therefore belong to you and to no one else. The Buddha teaches that because life is ruled by impermanence, things you crave will disappear from your life and things you reject will appear in your life. This is bound to happen at some point, no matter how much you struggle against it and what efforts you put into making your life predictable. You have very little control over the eventuality that someone will give you the attention you crave, or that you will have to undertake a work responsibility you would like to reject. You can do nothing about the certainty that craving will bring suffering as the things you crave disappear, and rejection will bring suffering as the things you reject appear. In short, you are walking the cycle of misery. This cycle can only be broken if you manage to reduce your attachment to your cravings and rejections, until this attachment finally ceases to exist. This, in fact, is the experience of unlearning we have discussed earlier.

Here and now exercise 7: Your cravings and rejections
Write down three of your most powerful cravings and three of your most powerful rejections. For the list of cravings, think of what you miss, but not necessarily in material terms. Think, for example, about power, safety, being cared for, caring for others, attention, compliments and similar needs. For the list of rejections think of those things you would do anything to get rid of.

Examples could be loneliness, being or not being at the centre of attention, being sad, etc. If you keep a journal, enter the list there. If not, keep the list in your mind.

Dependent and independent emotions

Your peace, your love and your happiness are all dependent. Not only do they depend on external input, this external input keeps changing as part of life's impermanence, throwing you in and out of love and peace. Love, peace, and happiness are all part of the polarity that dominates your life. Imagine them as a coin that has two sides; the coin of love invites the flip side of hate, the coin of peace invites the flip side of anxiety, the coin of happiness invites the flip side of sadness. All this happens because these feelings are dependent and powerfully linked to the Ego Formed Self. The love, happiness, and peace that are part of the undercurrent of your Authentic Self, are fundamentally different. They are independent. When you connect to this undercurrent while transcending your mind's reactions, the events that occur in the world around you have no impact on these feelings. They are born deep within your Authentic Self and are an integral part of it. Love, peace, and happiness reflect who you truly are; all you have to do is let go of the layers in which your Ego Formed Self is wrapped, and uncover this undercurrent. Engaging with change and dealing with your reactions to it are an important part of your unlearning journey. You have to identify the layers that cover the undercurrent, the automatic reactions that separate you from your Authentic Self. Moments of change are great teachers because they help you discover these barriers. When changes are underway, the reactive barriers automatically pop up and provide you with a wonderful opportunity to notice and explore them. The moment in which you notice your reaction to change is a gateway to expanding your awareness.

As part of the understanding of unconditional love, it is important to contemplate the difference between self-love and vanity. When our awareness connects with the Authentic Self, this is an invitation for self-love and a deep feeling awakens of compassion, acceptance, and warmth towards oneself. Notice that this is completely different than the Ego Formed Self based experience of vanity. Vanity is appreciation of oneself based on comparison with others; it is associated with a sense of superiority. Self-love, on the other hand, is unconditional and springs from within. The concepts of self-love and vanity are frequently confused. Self-love is perceived as vanity and as such is frowned at by society. The idea of sharing the words "I am beautiful" or "I love myself" with others tends to make us uncomfortable, simply because others could judge these words as vanity, and react accordingly. In fact, the ability to utter these words, and truly feel them in our hearts, is a fundamental aspect of one's growth. Self-love, with its deep acceptance and warmth, allows showing unconditional love for others, which is the spiritual experience of love.

Love may be explored from two different perspectives: psychological and spiritual. Psychology perceives love as a personal feeling, related to specific individuals under specific circumstances. The emotion we experience as love is the psychological expression of a variety of ego concepts, of needs and expectations that are being fulfilled. That is why the psychological experience of love is conditional and transient. But the spiritual concept of love is different. It is not personal. It is a manner of being that overflows your consciousness, regardless of whether or not the person in front of you fulfils your expectations or needs; in fact, there is no room for expectations or needs in this kind of experience. The spiritual experience of love is therefore unconditional and essentially stable; as long as you maintain an appropriate level of awareness, this experience of love is constantly waiting within you.

Weekly exercise 7: Engaging with change

In the table below, write down any changes you have noticed during the day. Focus on this table for a week and observe both the small changes ("your" chair in class or in a meeting room was taken by someone else) and the more serious ones (your friend has become distant). The changes may touch on any dimension of your life: personal, work, leisure, friends, romantic, or other. In the first column describe the change. Next to it describe the feelings it awoke in you. In the right hand column choose "craving" or "rejecting", to indicate which of the two basic reactions was triggered by the experience. If you repeat this exercise daily, you will discover the patterns of your reaction to changes in your life. Impermanence guarantees that changes of this kind are inevitable. Becoming aware of these reactions would therefore be an excellent starting point for future meditative work that will help you discard your rejections and cravings.

The Change	Feeling	Craving / Rejecting

Enlightenment is impermanent

One of the myths around enlightenment is that it is a durable experience that never changes. In reality, our awareness fluctuates; it is as impermanent as anything else. Note that the experience of enlightenment as a way of being does not change; it is always there, waiting for your awareness. As you practice meditation and keep growing, your awareness will extend and grow more consistent, yet it will continue to fluctuate. This means that your connection with the enlightened space, the Authentic Self, will also be subject to change. During my years of travelling and spiritual practice, I have met many individuals who have experienced enlightenment to varying extents. Some of the spiritual teachers I have met could even maintain that connection for long periods of time. And yet, I have never met individuals who experienced a steady, never-ending, enlightened state, where analysis by the mind never interferes at any point. We are human; it is no coincidence that we are born into the challenges of a body and a mind. Had we been meant to be pure spirits or entities of energy, we would have surely been embodied differently, and not be continuously challenged by our mind and body. We all contend with difficulties implanted within us: anger, frustration, jealousy, pain. Sometimes even joy brings discomfort. Spirituality does not resolve these difficulties. Frequently, the spiritual journey will take you even deeper into these feelings of discomfort. This is the meaning of being human. On your path towards enlightenment you will have to engage with such experiences. These challenges, which some might see as limitations, are the reason we are here. Our lives revolve around learning to live with, accept and relate to all that we are, including what we perceive as our personal limitations. We are not here to be perfect (whatever that means for you); we are here to deal with what we define as our imperfections and briefly touch the enlightened undercurrent as we transform. This transformation cannot be labelled. When we try to label it we fall into the trap of expectations and ego concepts. If you make enlightenment your benchmark, frustration will be your constant companion. Let go of seeking that enlightenment and you will feel great relief and freedom. It is the celebration of your liberation from ego concepts and expectations. I frequently observe spiritual seekers get deeply frustrated because they are not enlightened after many years of hard work. They are unable to recognise how entrapped they are in their own needs and concepts. Imagine the enlightened space as a road sign that indicates you have come in touch with your Authentic Self, and have been blessed with a glimpse of the experience of it. It does not matter if you reconnect to it next in a moment or in another lifetime. All you can do is continue your spiritual work here and now. And the freer this work is of expectations for enlightenment, the simpler you will find it to transform and grow.

Dear Human: You've got it all wrong. You didn't come here to master unconditional love. That is where you came from and where you'll return. You came here to learn personal love. Universal love. Messy love. Sweaty love. Crazy love. Broken love. Whole love. Infused with divinity. Lived through the grace of stumbling. Demonstrated through the beauty of... messing up. Often. You didn't come here to be perfect. You already are. You came here to be gorgeously human. Flawed and fabulous. And then to rise again into remembering. But unconditional love? Stop telling that story. Love, in truth, doesn't need ANY other adjectives. It doesn't require modifiers. It doesn't require the condition of perfection. It only asks that you show up. And do your best. That you stay present and feel fully. That you shine and fly and laugh and cry and hurt and heal and fall and get back up and play and work and live and die as YOU. It's enough. It's Plenty.
Courtney A. Walsh[36]

Lesson 8: Meditation and Freedom: Bringing It All Together

Thoughts and emotions

Psychological research has shown, via experiments and clinical observations, that it is not easy to tease apart our thoughts and our emotions.[37] Thoughts and emotions coexist, and we are unable to relate to them separately: "...Maslow emphasized the importance of integrating both cognition and emotion in a holistic way, consistent with contemporary research that shows the futility of disconnecting affect from thought, such as cognitive neuroscience findings that the two cannot be separated, and both codetermine behaviour".[38] For example, thoughts are accompanied by a certain emotional response; this emotional response is crucial for our decision making process and our ability to prioritise. Neuropsychology provides abundant support for this link.[39] People who have suffered brain damage that disconnected their thoughts from their emotions were examined to observe the effect of that disconnection. The results were startling: brain-damaged individuals found it very hard, almost impossible, to make decisions. When thought is not automatically accompanied by the emotional response it invites, the afflicted persons are locked in endless seemingly rational calculations. In the absence of emotion, they are not able to prioritise, and therefore cannot make decisions and achieve their goals. Take, for example, the simple task of choosing a restaurant. When your thoughts and feelings are disconnected, your mind keeps comparing variables such as the quality of the food, the place's atmosphere, the prices, and the location. But all these bits of information do not guarantee a decision. It takes emotions to link the thought about the atmosphere with pleasure, and to make you choose a particular restaurant, or to evoke aversion to the quality of the food and make you reject another.

Our thoughts and emotions are so powerfully intertwined that we rarely notice how connected they are. Before an exam we might be thinking "oh no, not an exam again, I don't like it" and "I don't do well in exams". These thoughts are bound to be accompanied by fear, anxiety, and other emotions that create considerable psychological discomfort. Thoughts and feelings are generated simultaneously, one reflecting the other. A closer look would reveal the fear reflected in the thoughts and the thoughts reflected in the fear. Not only do they appear simultaneously, they also feed on each other. Thoughts about failure and shame provoke feelings of fear and anxiety, while these feelings provoke thoughts about failure. This is a vicious circle, where your awareness is consumed by this thinking-emotional process. A similar process is often noticed with positive emotions. Thoughts of success and knowledge would lead to feelings such as inspiration, openness, and joy, and these feelings, for their part, would feed the thoughts. Once again, your awareness will be caught up in this cycle.

Emotions and bodily-sensations

Now that the thought-emotion link is clear, we can move on to the connection between emotions and bodily sensations. Emotions are subjective, internal experiences, and are linked with a variety of physiological reactions: "In the psychological literature, emotion has been defined as an individual's response to goal-relevant stimuli that includes behavioural, *physiological*, and experiential components".[40] A strong link exists between our emotions and our bodily responses. Psychologists use physiological criteria, such as the activity of the autonomic nervous system, to differentiate between emotions such as sadness, anger, joy, and grief.[41] These potential physiological responses may also impact your breathing, heart rate, and muscle tension. When this happens, you become aware of the changes in your body. Each of these changes directly provokes a sensation of its own. In other words, the emotions are linked with a physio-logical response that your awareness could recognise as a bodily sensation. Shortness of breath, rapid heartbeat, muscle tension – these are all detectable emotional indicators that you could attend to.

For most of its history, Western science has regarded our psyche and body as separate entities. As late as the last decades of the 20th century, the western scientific community viewed and researched human emotions and the human body as if they were separate. This point has important implications for the spiritual journey and for the potential tools that could help us walk this path. But first we should clearly understand the nature of the connection between emotions and body.

Imagine going out on a blind date. You may feel excited and a little apprehensive and you may even have butterflies in your stomach. Nervousness is frequently experienced in the stomach because certain physiological processes occur in the gut when we are stressed and nervous. These body-mind links work both ways; when we have indigestion, we often feel impatient and agitated. This reactive effect keeps accumulating as body and mind continuously provoke each other. To experience this body-mind link, I suggest you try the following short experiment: Imagine slicing a lemon and biting into it. Visualise lemon juice spilling into your mouth. You are probably salivating. Your thought has made your body respond.

A fascinating psychological study exemplifies this point.[42] The study researched the effect of positive emotions (caring/compassion) and negative emotions (anger/frustration/fear) on the body. Positive emotions, care and compassion, were induced using two different methods: In the first the participants were asked to direct their awareness to the area around the heart, where, according to most people, positive emotions are felt, and then focus on someone or something they love and feel compassion for. The second method involved watching a video of

Mother Teresa caring for homeless people in India and showing them her love. The participants were asked to let themselves experience freely and fully the emotions awakened during the viewing. Negative emotions of anger and fear were also induced in two different methods: In the first, the participants were asked to summon up and recall situations which tended to arouse in them negative emotions such as anger or frustration. Negative emotions were also induced by showing an edited video with difficult war scenes. The participants were instructed to experience any emotions aroused while watching the video freely and fully. The participants of the two groups were then asked to report their feelings, and the physiological effects of the positive or negative emotions were measured. The results showed that the physiological outcomes of positive emotions such as love, appreciation, and tranquillity, decreased the heart rates and relaxed the body in most of the participants. The physiological outcomes of the negative emotions reported by the other group, such as frustration, aggravation, and resentment, were higher heart rates, "a knot in the stomach", headaches, indigestion, muscle pains, and fatigue. These results clearly indicate the close connection between an emotion and the bodily sensations associated with it.

Psychological measurement 8: Body Awareness questionnaire

The Body Awareness Questionnaire[43] was developed to assess body sensations and body awareness. It measures your awareness of various bodily sensations and therefore mirrors your ability to observe the way thoughts and emotions are represented as sensations in your body.

Instructions: Listed below are a number of statements regarding your sensitivity to normal body processes. For each statement, select a number from 1 to 7 that best describes you.

1	Absolutely untrue of me
2	Moderately untrue of me
3	Slightly untrue of me
4	Neither true nor untrue of me
5	Slightly true of me
6	Moderately true of me
7	Absolutely true of me

1	I notice differences in the way my body reacts to various foods.	
2	I can always tell when I bump myself whether or not it will become a bruise.	
3	I always know when I've exerted myself to the point where I'll be sore the next day.	
4	I am always aware of changes in my energy level when I eat certain foods.	
5	I know in advance when I'm getting the flu.	
6	I know I'm running a fever without taking my temperature.	

7	I can distinguish between tiredness because of hunger and tiredness because of lack of sleep.	
8	I can accurately predict what time of day lack of sleep will catch up with me.	
9	I am aware of a cycle in my activity level throughout the day.	
10	I *don't* notice seasonal rhythms and cycles in the way my body functions.	
11	As soon as I wake up in the morning, I know how much energy I'll have during the day.	
12	I can tell when I go to bed how well I will sleep that night.	
13	I notice distinct body reactions when I am fatigued.	
14	I notice specific body responses to changes in the weather.	
15	I can predict how much sleep I will need at night in order to wake up refreshed.	
16	When my exercise habits change, I can predict very accurately how that will affect my energy level.	

17	There seems to be a "best" time for me to go to sleep at night.	
18	I notice specific bodily reactions to being over-hungry.	

Scoring: Final scores are obtained by reversing the score (1=7, 7=1, 2=6, 6=2, 3=5, 5=3, 4=4) of item 10 and summing up the scores of all 18 items. Your score is the arithmetic mean of the 18 items. Higher scores stand for higher body awareness.

Yoga, Psychology, and Spirituality

Yoga is one of the most relevant examples of the meeting point between body, mind, and emotions. The physical movement of the body combined with meditative awareness of the thoughts and emotions created in the mind, make a powerful path to self-liberation. The yogic philosophy and practice merge psychological and spiritual perspectives into a comprehensive system. Yoga originated in India around the 6th century BCE, as part of Hinduism. The word yoga, in Sanskrit, is derived from the root "yug", which is translated as "to yoke" (harness) or "to unite". By practicing, one harnesses yoga to unite the experiencer and experience, which is the state of the Authentic Self. Yoga allows the individual to gradually let go of the components of the Ego Formed Self by purifying body and mind. Contemplating the different branches of yoga is fascinating as it exemplifies the depth of yoga and the different paths it offers in our search for the Authentic Self. These branches of yoga include:

Rāja Yoga: Based upon meditation as the route to self-liberation. Patanjali's eight limbs of yoga[44] discussed below are the foundation of this branch of yoga.

Karma Yoga: The path of service. According to the idea of karma, our experiences of the present are linked to our actions in the past. Therefore karma yoga focuses on selflessness and actively serving others.

Bhakti Yoga: The path of devotion, cultivating acceptance, compassion, and love. Bhakti yoga considers every action, word and thought a potential opportunity to devote oneself to love and compassion.

Jnana Yoga: While Bhakti yoga focuses on the heart, Jnana focuses in a similar way on the mind. In this branch of yoga practitioners develop the intellect by devotedly studying the traditional yogic canon.

Hatha Yoga: The practice of Asanas (postures). The intention of hatha yoga is to purify the body and mind via the asanas.

The psychological and spiritual path is extremely personal. Each of us has an individual journey and applies different tools in order to regain freedom. The different branches of yoga offer different ways to apply the practice recognising the variety of paths one might choose from.

Within the yogic canon, the best example of the personal psycho-spiritual journey to freedom is found in the text of Patanjali's 196 Yoga Sutras (threads/lines). The sutras provide a series of short statements which, as they unfold, provide insights that allow growth and increased awareness. One of the most important sutras reads: **Yoga citta vritti nirodhah** (Chapter 1, v. 2), which translates as "yoga is the resolution of the agitations of the mind". The practice of yoga is a way of being that dissolves and resolves the ceaseless chatter and clatter of the mind, created by the Ego Formed Self, leaving the practitioner with the serenity of the Authentic Self. The next sutra reads: **Tada drastuh svarupe**

vasthanam (Chapter 1, v.3) – "Then the seer [awareness, consciousness] abides in its own nature". This transformational sutra indicates the process where the observer – awareness, consciousness – acts in accordance with its original form and nature; in other words, it transforms into the Authentic Self. The Ego Formed Self is dissolved and self transcendence, the essence of spirituality, takes its place. This is the state of connection to the undercurrent of the Authentic Self where unconditional bliss, love, compassion, peace, and acceptance are being experienced.

Patanjali's eight-limbs of yoga are the core of his yoga sutras, providing a structural framework for yoga practice. The eight limbs of yoga represent eight stages in one's path to enlightenment. These eight stages are a wonderful example of the meeting point between psychology and spirituality as they deal with various aspects of life, beginning with a psychological process that gradually transforms and supports spiritual change. This eight-stage psycho-spiritual journey goes well beyond the physical practice of hatha yoga. We frequently think of yoga in relation to a physical posture: "Postures are taught as ends in themselves merely to heal an illness, reduce stress, or look better. The fact that these postures are a foundation for self-realization is generally ignored. Yoga is often thought of as the headstand, the lotus posture, or another pretzel-like pose. "[45] Being a yogi, a practitioner of yoga, involves a way of life that advocates spiritual growth, ethical living, self-discipline, and awareness. The eight-limbs of yoga are a step-by-step manual that leads to awakening through yoga. The first limb is *Yama;* this stage provides ethical standards, and deepens integrity and authenticity. As part of Yama one follows Ahimsa (non-violence) and Satya (truthfulness), fundamental states of mind that are essential for one's self-growth. Creating this initial relationship with others and with the environment is the beginning of the yogic path and is followed by the second limb, *Niyama.* This limb teaches spiritual observation and self-discipline and includes

Santosha (contentment) and Swadhayaya (self-study). Niyama illustrates the relationship with one's own self and therefore is a more developed stage than the first limb's relationship with the environment. The third limb is *Asana;* this stage emphasises the importance of physical postures. The body, according to yogic tradition, is the temple of the spirit and as such is important to our spiritual journey. As the yogi practices asanas, different parts of his body become the focal point of his awareness, developing discipline and concentration. Breath control and awareness are the foundations of the fourth stage, *Pranayama.* Gaining mastery over the breathing process allows experiencing the link between breath, body, mind, and emotions, enhancing self-awareness. These first four stages refine self-development and prepare the practitioner for the final four stages, which go deeper into meditation. The fifth limb is *Pradyahara* where withdrawal or sensory transcendence is being taught. The yogi is aware of the external world and yet is able to avoid reacting to sensory input. To illustrate this stage let us look into a study that compares the startle response of an experienced meditator and a control group (non-meditators) to loud noises played while the participants are in an fMRI machine (measuring brain activity).[46] The results indicated that the control group's physiological and facial responses to the loud noises were significantly stronger compared with those of the meditator. In other words, the meditator applied pradyahara skills which allowed him to be aware of the loud noises while remaining detached and significantly less reactive to them. The sixth limb is *Dharana;* this stage teaches how to concentrate on a single mental object. A clear link exists between each stage that prepares us for the following one; it would be very difficult to keep one's attention focused on a single object without pradyahara practice, as attention would keep wandering by reacting to external stimuli and therefore would be pulled away from the Dharana focal point of concentration. The seventh stage is *Meditation;* here your attention is focused without a focal point, in an open manner. The mind is still and quiet at this point and deep peace is experienced. This peace leads to the eighth and final limb of yoga, which is *Samadhi*, where the yogi self-transcends and all aspects of the Ego Formed Self fade away. A deep feeling of bliss and interconnectedness with all living beings is experienced at this stage. This is the final step of the yogic transformation and it represents the enlightenment that we discussed earlier in the book. Notice how gradual this invitation for transformation is; it begins with the psychological aspects of values and attitudes the yogi changes, step by step, and deepens the practice into the spiritual realm by shifting into meditation practice. The beauty of this process lies in that the early limbs, which focus on psychological change, are necessary in order to gradually move towards the later limbs that focus on the spiritual, transcendent, and meditative experience. Again we see the strong link between psychology and spirituality and realize that one is fundamental for the development of the other. The power of this yogic journey lies in the holistic usage of human dimensions: body, mind, and spirit are integrated in the creation of a transformative way of being.

Thoughts, emotions and bodily reactions: the link

By now, a link has been established between thoughts and emotions, and between emotions and the body. All three are closely linked. "We can no longer think of the emotions as having less validity than physical, material substances, but instead must see them as cellular signals that are involved in the process of translating information into physical reality, literally transforming mind into matter. Emotions are at the nexus between matter and mind, going back and forth between the two and influencing both"[39]. Thoughts-emotions-bodily sensations; a powerful triangle that works in a synchronized way. Think of them as parts of one wave; when the wave rises, they all rise, when the wave falls, they all fall. Like three gearwheels in an old-fashioned watch, connected to each other, the movement of each wheel also moving the others, and with them the hands of the watch. In other words, every change in our thoughts, emotions or body, creates a ripple that affects the other two. Powerful or gentle, a movement in each of the three will impact the other two. They go hand in hand.

Relevance to your spiritual journey

How is the link between thoughts, emotions and the body relevant to your spiritual journey? In lesson 3 we already discussed the importance of non-reactive attention. We know now that it has an extremely important role in breaking our attachment to thought patterns and releasing us from them. Now that we know that emotions are reflections of thoughts, we could observe our feelings rather than our thoughts.

Our emotions have the capacity to take over our awareness in the same way as our thoughts do. When we are engulfed by an emotion, we are rarely present, and this lack of awareness creates a powerful attachment to that emotion, and we find it almost impossible to let our awareness be an observer. The emotion and your immediate reaction become entangled and disconnect you from the moment. Take for example a moment of anger. If the ego concepts that trigger it are powerful, you will literally disappear when it flares up. Your awareness will be swallowed up by the emotion and it will take some time before you regain control. Many New Age theories maintain that we should express our feelings in full; this may be true but not entirely correct. Expressing emotions is perfectly fine as long as you are able to retain the non-reactive attention we have discussed earlier. If you react to the emotion you are experiencing, that is, if you are not fully present, the emotion will take over your awareness, and generate a series of reactions. As already mentioned, reacting is the fuel that feeds the thoughts and the emotions, perpetuates them, and helps them grow. By reacting you start a chain of memories, thoughts, and expectations; these link with other emotions of hurt and pain, which themselves connect with further thoughts of unfulfilled needs, and so on and so forth. This whirlwind of reactions is based upon your non-presence. The alternative is to observe the emotion in a non-reactive manner, as we have been trying to do with our thoughts. You are aware that you are experiencing anger, but you are able to perceive it for what it is: an emotion that will come and go. You are the observer on the hill, not rejecting the anger or pushing it away. Remember, pushing away your anger is just another ego concept saying that the emotion is wrong and should be removed as quickly as possible. A reaction of this kind will feed the emotion just as any other reaction would. You may be able to push an emotion away from your awareness, but it will continue to bubble within you even more powerfully, and will develop into a stronger ego concept.

Emotions are provoked at specific moments; when we react to them they continue to exist for extended periods of time, long after they have become irrelevant. If you observe an emotion that arose in response to a difficulty without reacting to it, it would fade away and let you move on with your life. But this rarely happens. One emotion leads to a series of irrelevant ones. This chain can only be broken by meditative presence that would pull you away from reacting to the emotion and fuelling it. Therefore, do not reject the emotion or push it away. Create a new kind of relationship with it, the kind that takes you off the merry go round of anger, frustration, and guilt.

Consistent non-reactive observation would bring about growth that will be manifested in two ways:

1 *Intensity* of the emotion: Negative emotions such as anger, and their accompanying bodily sensations, will lose much of their intensity.

2 *Duration* of the emotion: Negative emotions and their

accompanying bodily sensations would not last. If in the past a certain event made you steam in anger for hours, you will notice that with practice you will regain your calm much sooner. Every hour you gain this way is an hour of tranquillity. This is a great reward for your practice.

Observing? How?

Many of my students report that they have difficulty observing their often abstract emotions. Where is anxiety located? How can you focus on fear? Let us take advantage of this difficulty and turn it into a wonderful opportunity for non-reactive observation of your bodily sensations. We have already established that the body and its sensations mirror our emotional and cognitive responses. Therefore, if you have difficulty observing your thoughts or your emotions, you could observe instead your body. *Let your body be the screen on which the movie that runs in your mind is displayed.* Whatever this movie is made of – thoughts, expectations, desires, feelings – it will be represented by a corresponding bodily sensation. As you observe each of these sensations without reacting to it, you establish a non-attached relationship with it, and at the same time break your attachment to the thoughts and emotions that are related to it. Let me give you an example. On your way to meet friends you may recall certain promises they have never fulfilled and your disappointment with them. These thoughts are accompanied by feelings of anger and hurt. Your body may respond by tenseness in your stomach or a certain tightening in your chest. This is where you apply the meditative skills you have acquired by regular practice of meditation; you direct your attention to your stomach or chest without reaction, and observe the sensations you felt in them gradually fade away. The point is that focusing our attention on bodily sensations is easier than observing our fleeting thoughts or emotions, which are less concrete and defined. Note, however, that each of us has different strengths and skills. You may discover that focusing on thoughts, for example, is easier *for you*. If that is the case – do not fight it; just keep your attention where it is easiest to focus. Remember, no matter which of the three you choose to focus on, be sure to attend to it non-reactively, and it will affect the others. They are linked.

Here and now exercise 8(A): Emotions and sensations

This exercise invites you to experience the strong link between your emotions and the bodily sensations that accompany them. First sit or lie down comfortably. Make sure that your muscles are relaxed, and your body is calm and receptive. Close your eyes and recall one of your best experiences. It can be the moment when your child was born, a magical sunset on the beach, your first kiss with the person you love – anything that truly and deeply moved you in a positive way. Try to visualise it as vividly as you can, and keep the picture in your mind. Allow yourself some time to notice the details. Let yourself be engulfed by waves of delightful emotions: happiness, pride, joy, ecstasy. Spend as much time as you need to make the event come alive in your mind, and feel the accompanying emotions as vividly as possible. After you have dedicated a couple of minutes to the event and to the positive emotions it triggered, scan your body with your awareness. Observe different parts of your body and notice what is happening in them. Do certain areas feel more open, receptive, or relaxed? Do you have any special sensations somewhere, such as a tingling? Make a mental note of your bodily sensations and your emotions at that specific moment. This exercise is meant to give you a glimpse of the meeting point between thoughts, emotions, and the sensations you experience. You could also try the same exercise with a negative event. This will give you an opportunity to compare the sensations triggered by a positive emotion with those triggered by a negative one.

Here and now exercise 8(B): The rag-doll technique

The powerful link between the tension or relaxation of the muscles and our thoughts and emotions could be used to calm down the mind by relaxing the body. A simple example of this is the rag-doll technique. Close your eyes, take a deep breath and, as you exhale, completely relax your body. While you release the air soften every muscle in your body starting from your head and jaw, moving to your shoulders, back, hands and legs. See if you can do that very quickly, switching from a state of tension where the muscles are strained, sometimes unconsciously, into complete relaxation of the muscles. Make your body completely soft and tensionless, like that of a rag-doll. As you practice this simple but powerful technique you will notice the impact this shift has on your mind. When the body's muscles are tense the mind reflects the same stress and rigidity, which could easily lead to rumination and psychological discomfort. On the other hand, when you let go and enter the rag-doll state, the mind relaxes and fills with peace. This is a practical technique that could be practiced frequently and regularly until you are able to apply it without any conscious effort. Whenever you recognise stress and rigidity in your body you automatically invite the rag-doll state for a few breaths, find peace and quiet, and only then return to whatever you were doing.

The art of non-reaction

Your mind is like the sand on the beach. Every time you react to a situation with a certain thought and emotion, you dig an ego concept hole a little deeper. Your mind has an amazing capacity to remember, and memories keep building up in it. Every time you react to a situation with an ego concept means that when a similar event happens next, this ego concept will promptly enter into action and will control your awareness for a slightly longer time. Psychological research of attitudes confirms this observation. The research shows that the attitudes we adopt most frequently and most easily are those that come first to your mind and they are the ones that have the greatest influence on our behaviour. In other words, attitudes, just like ego concepts, survive because they are part of a loop that feeds upon itself and keeps getting stronger; whenever you adopt an attitude you let it become slightly more available in your mind, and strengthen its influence on your behaviour.

What happens, then, when you do not react? Non-reactive attention to a thought, an emotion, or a sensation is helpful in two ways: First, it prevents your attention from getting entrenched in the "hole in the sand", because by not reacting you break the cycle that strengthens the involved ego concept. No less important, every time you refrain from reacting, you throw some sand back into the hole. Whatever you are feeling is not fuelled by your reactive attention and your attachment to it is reduced. In the future, this emotion will have a weaker grip on your awareness. With consistent practice, the hole will be gradually filled up until it completely disappears. When you reach that point your jealousy, frustration, expectation or need will no longer have any power over your attention. As the hole closes up, you will also find it easier to remain present in the face of that particular issue. Imagine, for example, that a colleague asks you personal questions at work that trigger a reaction. The ego concept behind it may be "people at work should mind their own businesses", the accompanying thought is "he is so annoying, sticking his nose into other people's business", coupled with irritation or feelings of disrespect that will be reflected in certain bodily sensations. Every time you bring your attention to this person's questions and allow your mind to react, you dig the hole slightly deeper and guarantee that next time, milder prying will trigger the same reaction. On the other hand, as you begin to observe the ego concept non-reactively, or even smile gently at its struggle to take control of your awareness and make you react, you are detaching yourself from it and the hole is being filled.

Next time the effect of the ego concept will be slightly less intense, and you will find it slightly easier not to react. The important change is that by consistently observing your self you will be able to move away from the experience smoothly, peacefully, with no anger or drama.

Weekly exercise 8(A): Body awareness

This week we will practice the chakra meditation for ten minutes every day. In Hindu thought, chakras are centres of energy that pass across the body; we will be focusing on seven central chakras that pass between the lower end of the spine and the top of the head. In chakra meditation you are asked to focus your attention on a particular area that represents a certain chakra in your body, and observe your bodily sensations in that area.

Whether or not you accept the idea that chakras or centres of energy run across your body, you can use them as focal points to examine bodily sensations. We will practice non-reactive attention to bodily sensations by going over the chakras. You can practice this meditation lying down, sitting, or standing up. Choose the position that is most comfortable for you. Begin the practice with three deep breaths. Exhale slowly, letting your muscles relax. While you meditate, place both your palms on the area of the chakra; this will make it easier for you to direct your attention at that area and connect to the sensations there. Devote about one minute to each chakra and let your awareness climb up your body. One minute is about the time needed to take five deep, slow, breaths, but do not be too preoccupied with the time or the number of breaths; when you feel that the number of breaths is approximately right, move on to the next chakra.

Place both palms on your lower abdomen, just above your genitals, around the height of the end of your spine. This is the area of the first chakra, also called the Root chakra. Close your eyes and allow your awareness to ride your breath as it goes down into the first chakra. Observe your sensations in this area.

Can you recognise any of them? Is there tension or is there openness? Do you feel a movement? You might experience other sensations such as contraction and expansion, pressure, pulling, heat and coldness, lightness and heaviness, tingling, pain, or numbness. Whatever you recognise is perfectly fine. Remember, you are pursuing non-reactive attention and should do absolutely nothing with the sensations you discover. Simply bring your awareness to the area and observe. You may feel nothing, which is perfectly fine as well; focus on the feeling of nothing. Any sensation or non-sensation may shift and change as you observe it. If this happens, simply make a note of the change with complete presence, because that is the transformation your awareness and presence bring about. After five slow breaths into your first chakra, move your palms a little higher, just below your bellybutton. This is the second chakra, also called Hara. Repeat the same observation process for five breaths. The third chakra, called the Solar Plexus, is located two inches below the breastbone; place both palms there, take five slow breaths, and observe the sensations in this area. The fourth chakra is the Heart. Place both palms on your heart and bring your full attention to that area. The fifth chakra is the Throat; place both palms on your throat, bring your awareness to that area, and observe. The sixth chakra is called the Third Eye and is located in the middle of your forehead between your eyebrows. The seventh and final chakra is called the Crown and is located at the top of your head. When you reach the seventh chakra spend an extra half minute there, that is, seven slow breaths in total, and then descend, passing again through all the chakras until you reach the first chakra. As you descend, remain in each chakra for about 30 seconds, the time of two slow breaths. When you have completed the round, let your hands fall to your sides or place them on your heart, and take a few breaths before you open your eyes.

Weekly exercise 8(B): Reaction to events

In your second weekly exercise, you are asked to complete the following table:

Event	Thought	Emotion	Sensation
Example: I stumbled and fell in the middle of a crowded street	I'm so clumsy	Humiliation	A burning sensation in my heart

Enter in the table the events that occurred during the day, and the reactive thought, emotion and sensation that accompanied them. You may enter the details in the table immediately after the event or later. You may write down as many events as you remember; try to describe at least one event per day.

Combined, these two exercises will help you stay aware all day long. The first exercise will increase your sensitivity to bodily sensations and the second one will help you link daily events with the reactions that accompany them (thoughts, emotions and sensations). As you focus your attention and try to find these reactions, you will gradually notice that every moment incorporates all three of them unless it is transcended. You will recognise, on an experiential level, how a simple refusal could tighten your chest, while a smile would expand your heart.

Learn how to bring your attention automatically to these sensations. With time, you will no longer need to remind yourself to do it; your awareness will identify any sensation rising in your body and attend to it. These sensations will slowly become your friends and you will find in them a convenient focal point that continuously invites you to be present.

Another significant change that you will gradually experience is the ability to notice much subtler sensations. The Buddha said that whatever occurs in the mind always manifests itself in the body. Every single moment shoots diverse sensations through our body. Most of them go unnoticed because we are not sufficiently sensitive to them, and our awareness does not recognise them. Some thought-emotion-sensation patterns are very powerful and cannot be missed or ignored; a thought may be like a shout in your mind, an emotion may vibrate with intensity, and a sensation may be almost physically painful. Cases such as these may be related to certain traumas. But other sensations may be much subtler. They are not as intense and therefore go undetected. The more you practice the less will your sensations pass under the radar of your awareness. When you have reached this stage, less powerful patterns will also disappear slowly.

Life-long exercise: Going deeper into your authentic self

The journey offered by this book is not an eight-week process, it is life-long. The eight weeks, with their ideas and exercises, would significantly enhance this journey, and yet your practice does not end until you breathe your last breath. When you are through reading this book, I would like you to take with you my final and most important message: Make sure to continue meditating on a daily basis. Meditation is the experiential foundation for the process of change described in this book. Entering into a deeper meditative state is essential to enhancing the quality of awareness that allows you to become united with your authentic self.

Continue practicing meditation regularly once or twice a day for at least 10 minutes per session. You may decide to choose the breathing meditation, or any other technique of the eight described, or you could switch between techniques, practicing every day the one that feels right for that day. The actual technique is not as important as the regular, consistent, practice. It is this practice that will gradually transform you, and make the freedom of awareness grow into a feeling of deep contentedness.

Final words

If I had to choose one word to describe the spiritual journey, I would say that it is personal, more than anything else. Each and every one of us faces different challenges, and goes through unique experiences. We have very little control over the events that actually occur along the adventure we call life. Whenever we think that we have made some progress and we now see life as it really is – life has a way of slapping us in the face and showing us that we still have so much more to learn. Growth is endless. Your final moment of growth will be your last breath. This may sound discouraging, but in truth I find it quite exhilarating. It means that there is always space for us to expand, to realize another part of our amazing and endless true potential.

But we should keep in mind that this takes hard work. Those who think that spiritual growth is mostly about burning incense and sitting cross-legged for ten minutes a day have never truly challenged themselves. Daily confrontation with the games you play, the masks you put on, and your defence strategies is exhausting. And yet, I cannot think of a more rewarding experience. The moments in which you realise that you are free of the grip of a years-long pattern, that a certain situation no longer breaks your heart as it used to in the past, and that criticism no longer fills your stomach with fear – these are moments of victory. Because freedom really means gaining control over your self, the self that has imprisoned you and has been narrowing your experience of life. The feeling of progress towards becoming your Authentic Self is profound joy. In the lessons included in this book, psychology and spirituality were interwoven, jointly creating an extremely valuable tool for you to use in your journey of growth. Growing is impossible unless you get to know your self (psychology) and experience transcendence (spirituality). Bringing them together and utilizing their generous offer for growth to the fullest is a celebration of freedom. This will not happen of its own accord. It requires hard work, true dedication, and regular practice.

- To break life-long patterns ego concepts must be dissolved.
- To dissolve ego concepts meditative skills are required.
- And it takes dedicated practice to master the skills of meditation.

There is no way to bypass this hard work. No one is able to set you free by chanting holy words over your head. Your path to growth is yours to walk. No one can walk it for you or carry you through the journey. Others can only inspire you and offer you certain ideas and instructions. This is your kitchen, your kitchenware, and your cake to bake. All I can do is offer my recipes. Make sure to adapt these ideas and instructions to your own needs. There is no proven or perfect recipe for this growth process. Look for your own voice in every step that you make; *it has to be your own.*

My students tell me that their practice is sometimes slack because they are "lazy". I don't believe in laziness. Fear is more often than not the thing that holds us back. Fear makes us promise to meditate "tomorrow", or say "this exercise is not very important, I'll find another time to practice it". What is it that frightens us so much? We are afraid to realise who we truly are, to admit that the game we are playing is based on an illusion, and to accept that our self is at the centre of this illusion. These ideas are intimidating, and to actually act upon them is even scarier because it means breaking the rules of the life game that you have been playing until now. Once you admit this to yourself and really see it all, you will have no choice but to reconsider your priorities, weigh your choices, and rethink your life. Therefore, it takes courage to set out on the spiritual journey, the courage to really look at your self and ask the right questions. And as you watch the walls of the mental prison you have created around your awareness crumble, you will need courage not to run away but stand still and watch the illusion disappear. Once you reach this point, all that remains is awareness, the awareness that made the illusion disappear, and the awareness that was left behind once the illusion was gone. Awareness Is Freedom.

To read more about Itai Ivtzan's work:
www.AwarenessIsFreedom.com

References

1   Ivtzan, I., Chan, C. P. L., Gardner, H. E., & Prashar, K. (2011). Linking religion and spirituality with psychological wellbeing: Examining self actualisation, meaning in life, and personal growth initiative. *Journal of Religion and Health, 51,* 13-30.

2   Christensen, I. P., Wagner, H. L., and Halliday M. S. (2001). Instant Notes Psychology. New Delhi: Viva Books.

3   Thompson, M. M., Naccarato, M. E., Parker, K. C. H., & Moskowitz, G. B. (2001). The Personal Need for Structure and Personal Fear of Invalidity Measures: Historical perspectives, current applications, and future directions. In G. B. Moskowitz (Ed.), *Cognitive Social Psychology: The Princeton Symposium on the Legacy and Future of Social Cognition.* London: Lawrence Erlbaum Associates.

4   Jane, R. (1994). Seth Speaks: The Eternal Validity of the Soul (Seth Book). New World Library.

5   Brewer, J. A., Mallik, S., Babuscio, T. A., Nich, C., Johnson, H. E., Deleone, C. M., Minnix-Cotton, C. A., Byrne, S.A., Kober, H., Weinstein, A. J., Carroll, K.M., & Rounsaville, B. J. (2011). "Mindfulness Training for smoking cessation: results from a randomized controlled trial." *Drug and Alcohol Dependence, 119,* 72-80.

6   Grossman, P., Niemann, L., Schmidt, S., Walach, H. (2004). Mindfulness-based stress reduction and health benefits: A meta-analysis. *Journal of Psychosomatic Research, 57*(1), 35-43.

7   Chiesa, A., & Serretti, A. (2009). Mindfulness-based stress reduction for stress management in healthy people: A review and meta-analysis. *Journal of Alternative and Complementary Medicine, 15(5),* 593.

8   Brown, K. W., & Ryan, R. M. (2003). The Benefits of Being Present: Mindfulness and its Role in Psychological Well-

Being. *Journal of Personality and Social Psychology, 84(4),* 822-48.

9   Carmody, J., & Baer, R. A. (2008). Relationships between mindfulness practice and levels of mindfulness, medical and psychological symptoms and well-being in a mindfulness-based stress reduction program. *Journal of Behavioral Medicine, 31,* 23-33.

10   Lazar, S. W., Kerr, C. E., Wasserman, R. H., Gray, J. R., Greve, D. N., Treadway, M. T., et al. (2005). Meditation experience is associated with increased cortical thickness. *Neuroreport, 16(17),* 1893-1997.

11   Desbordes, G., Negi, L. T., Pace, T. W., Wallace, B. A., Raison, C. L., & Schwartz, E. L. (2012). Effects of mindful-attention and compassion meditation training on amygdala response to emotional stimuli in an ordinary, non-meditative state. *Frontiers in Human Neuroscience, 1(6),* 292.

12   Shapiro, D. H. (1982). Overview: Clinical and physiological comparison of meditation with other self-control strategies. *American Journal of Psychiatry, 139,* 267-274.

13   MacLean, K. A., Ferrer, E., Aichele, S. R., Bridwell, D. A., Zanesco, A. P., Jacobs, T. L., King, B. G., Rosenberg, E. L., Sahdra, B. K., Shaver, P. R., Wallace,B. A., Mangun, G. R., & Saron, C. D. (2010). *Intensive meditation training leads to improvements in perceptual discrimination and sustained attention. Psychological Science, 21(6),* 829-839.

14   Tang, Y., Lu, Q., Geng, X., Stein, E. A., Yang, Y., Posner, M. I. (2010). Short-term meditation induces white matter changes in the anterior cingulate. *Proceedings of the National Academy of Sciences, 107(35),* 15649-15652.

15   Zeidan, F., Johnson, S. K., Diamond, B. J., David, Z., & Goolkasian, P. (2010). Mindfulness meditation improves cognition: Evidence of brief mental training. *Consciousness and Cognition, 19(2),* 597-605.

16   Robitschek, C. (1998). Personal growth initiative: The

construct and its measure. *Measurement and Evaluation in Counseling and Development, 30,* 183–198.

17 Wachs, K. T., Meade, A. E., & Cordova, J. V. (2008). The Relational Acceptance Questionnaire (RAQ): A Validation Study. Poster presented at the 42nd annual meeting of the Association of Cognitive and Behavioral Therapists, Orlando, FL.

18 Wu Wei Wei. (1963). Ask the awakened. London: Routledge.

19 Ivtzan, I., & Conneely, R. (2009). Androgyny in the mirror of self actualisation and spiritual health. *The Open Psychology Journal, 2,* 58-70.

20 Metzinger, T. (2010). The Ego Tunnel: The Science of the Mind and the Myth of the Self. NY: Basic Books.

21 Baggini, J. (2012). *The Ego Trick.* London: Granta.

22 Ivtzan, I., Gardner, H. E., & Smailova, Z., (2011). Mindfulness meditation and curiosity: The contributing factors to wellbeing and the process of closing the self-discrepancy gap. *International Journal of Wellbeing, 1*(3), 316-326.

23 Wayne, L. (2013, January 7). Message from Wayne. Advaita Fellowship. Retrieved from http://www.advaita.org/newslet tertemplate/news1110.html.

24 Hwang, J. Y., Plante, T., & Lackey, K. (2008). The development of the santa clara brief compassion scale: An abbreviation of sprecher and fehr's compassionate love scale. *Pastoral Psychology, 56,* 421–428.

25 French, C. C., & Richards, A. R. (1993). 'Clock this! An everyday example of schema-driven error in memory', *British Journal of Psychology, 84,* 249-53.

26 Bartlett, F. C. (1932/reissued 1995). *Remembering.* Cambridge: Cambridge University Press.

27 Bargh, J. A., Chen, M., & Burrows, L. (1996). Automaticity of social behavior: Direct effects of trait construct and stereotype activation on action. *Journal of Personality and*

Social Psychology, 71(2), 230-244.

28 Blais, M. R. & Vallerand, R. J. (1991). *Construction et validation de l'Échelle des Perceptions d'Autonomie dans les Domaines de Vie*. Université du Québec à Montréal, Canada. Unpublished manuscript.

29 Killingsworth, M. A., & Gilbert, D. T. (2010). A wandering mind is an unhappy mind. *Science, 330,* 932.

30 Baer, R. A., Smith, G. T., Hopkins, J., Krietemeyer, J., & Toney, L. (2006). Using self-report assessment methods to explore facets of mindfulness. *Assessment, 13,* 27-45.

31 Fredrickson, B. L., Cohn, M. A., Coffey, K. A., Pek, J., & Finkel, S. M. (2008). Open hearts build lives: Positive emotions, induced through loving-kindness meditation, build consequential personal resources. *Journal of Personality and Social Psychology, 95,* 1045-1062.

32 Geer, J. H., & Maisel, E. (1972). Evaluating the effects of the prediction-control confound. *Journal of Personality and Social Psychology, 23,* 314-319.

33 Steger, M. F., Frazier, P., Oishi, S., & Kaler, M. (2006). The Meaning in Life Questionnaire: Assessing the presence of and search for meaning in life. *Journal of Counseling Psychology, 53,* 80-93.

34 Kabat-Zinn, J. (1994). Wherever you go there you are: Mindfulness meditations in everyday life. New York: Hyperion.

35 Osho (1981). Take it Easy: v. 1: Talks on Zen Buddhism. NY: Osho International Foundation.

36 Walsh, C. A. (2014, September 13). *Dear Human*. Retrieved from http://www.squeezingthestars.com/

37 Dolan, R. J. (2002). Emotion, cognition, and behavior. *Science, 298,* 1191-1194.

38 Friedman, H. & Robbins, B. D. (2012). The Negative Shadow Cast by Positive Psychology: Contrasting Views and Implications of Humanistic and Positive Psychology on

Resiliency. *The Humanistic Psychologist* , *40(1)*, 87-102.

39 Gray, J. R., Braver, T. S., & Raichle, M. E. (2002). Integration of emotion and cognition in the lateral prefrontal cortex. *Proceedings of the National Academy of the Sciences, 99(6)*, 4115-4120.

40 Pert, C. (1999). *Molecules of Emotion: Why You Feel the Way You Feel.* New-York: Simon and Schuster.

41 Ekman, P., Levenson, R. W., & Friesen, W. V. (1983). Autonomic nervous system activity distinguishes among emotions. *Science, 221 (4616)*, 1208–1210.

42 Rein, G., Atkinson, M., & McCraty, R. (1995). The Physiological and Psychological Effects of Compassion and Anger. *Journal of Advancement in Medicine, 8(2)*, 87-105.

43 Shields, S. A., Mallory, M. E., & Simon, A. (1989). The Body Awareness Questionnaire: Reliability and validity. *Journal of Personality Assessment, 53*, 802-815.

44 Satchidananda, S. (2012). *Yoga Sutras of Patanjali.* Integral Yoga Publications.

45 Chauhan, S. (1992). Role of yogic exercises in the withdrawal symptoms of drug-addicts. *Yoga Mimamsa, 30*, 21–23.

46 Levenson, R. W., *Ekman*, P., & *Ricard*, M. (2012). Meditation and the startle response: A case study. *Emotion, 12(3)*, 650-658.